KELLY HOPPEN
Style

Kelly Hop

S
Dedicated with love and affection. xx

pen Style

The Golden Rules
of Design

Kelly Hoppen

Text by Helen Chislett
Photography by Vincent Knapp

Bulfinch Press
New York · Boston · London

Bulfinch Press

Hachette Book Group USA,
237 Park Avenue
New York, NY 10169

Visit our Web site at www.bulfinchpress.com

First United States Paperback Edition: September 2006
Third printing, 2007

First printed in Great Britain in 2004 by Jacqui
Small, an imprint of Aurum Press
ISBN: 978-0-8212-5849-1

Hardcover Library of Congress Control Number 2004102598

Design by Lawrence Morton

PRINTED IN SINGAPORE

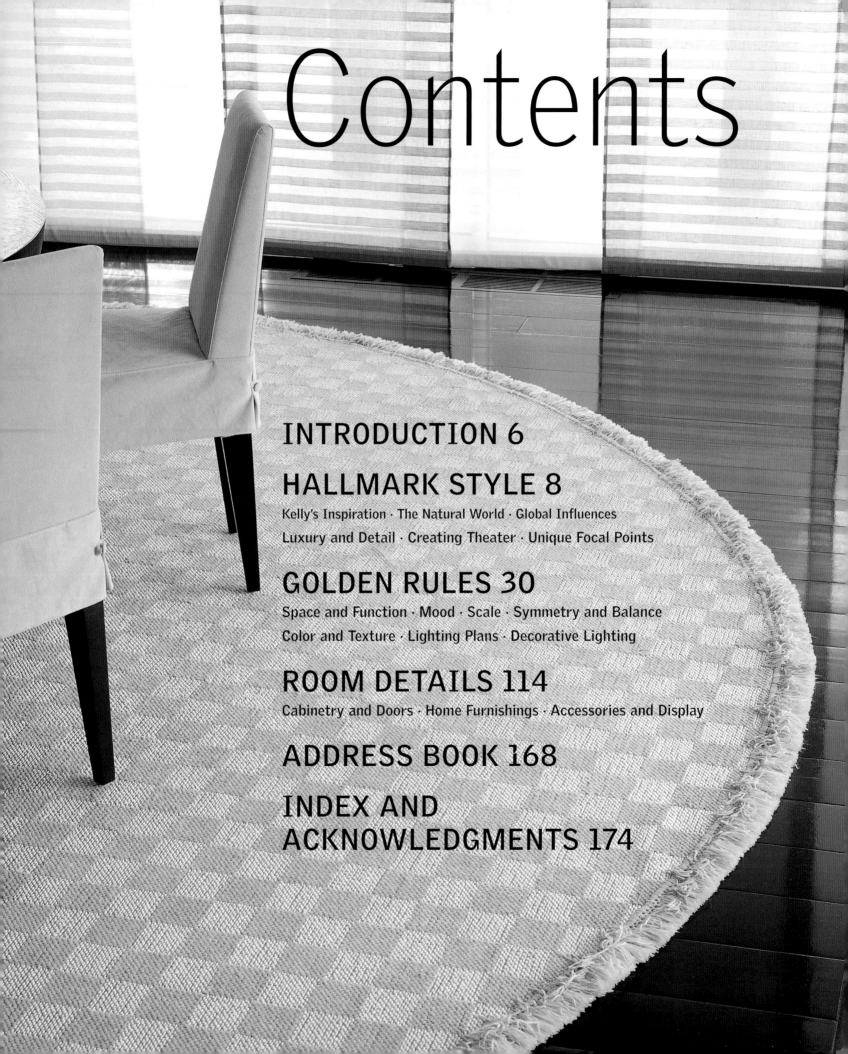

Contents

Introduction

One of the wonderful things about producing a book is that it makes you stop and think. There has to be a time for reflection, a chance to stop and look at interior design and consider what is really important right at this moment. Interestingly, it has brought into sharp focus the fact that I feel very differently about my home than the way I felt three years ago. My last book, *Close Up*, was launched on 11 September 2001, possibly the blackest date in recent history. Until then, interior design was focused on creating a look that was out to impress. But from that day on, something changed. We realized that to go home was a privilege not a given. People began to spend more time at home and to turn those homes into cocoons of security and warmth. Clients no longer demanded interiors built on the wow factor – instead they touched on different values, how they wanted to feel: safe, comfortable, relaxed and happy. Having the so-called "perfect show house" no longer mattered. Having a home that really was a home did. And I find myself completely in tune with that. How a room looks is important, but it must also reflect you and your family and be grounded in reality. It is how you feel when you are in it – whether eating, talking, reading or sleeping. The art of design is now about using space, light, color and texture to promote good feelings. The biggest compliment anyone can pay me is to walk into one of my rooms and say it has a positive influence on their mood. I am convinced that a calm, quiet and harmonious interior can be as beneficial to health as a sensible diet and regular exercise.

I am also aware that mine is a look that has spawned a thousand imitators. Yet few really tap into the essence of what I do. This book is for those who love my style, yet can't quite capture the look when they try it. I have tried to explain my golden rules of decorating, gathered from over 25 years of experience. Each chapter focuses on a different aspect of the design process. For example, Space and Function is about assessing the potential of a room before making any choices about lighting or furniture. From here on, subsequent chapters examine everything from Color and Texture, Cabinetry and Doors, to Home Furnishings and Accessories and Display.

All books are a journey and this has been a particularly interesting one. When I design, it comes straight from the heart, so it goes against the grain to sit down and analyze what I have done and why. The experience of running my own design school has helped me find ways of communicating my ideas and made me far more aware of why one idea works brilliantly and another doesn't, why some people struggle and others appear to do things effortlessly. This book is for all those who love their homes and pour their hearts into them. I know exactly how you feel.

Hallmark style

NATURAL   LUXURIOUS   GLOBAL

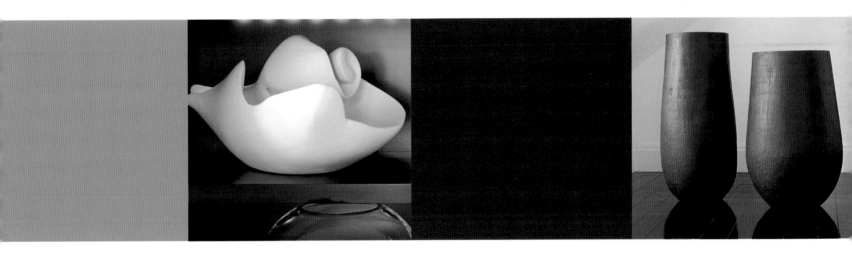

THEATER   UNIQUE FOCAL POINTS

THIS SECTION IS ABOUT THE INFLUENCES AND
INSPIRATIONS THAT ARE INHERENT IN MY DESIGN
WORK. SOME ARE OBVIOUS, OTHERS LESS SO.
WHAT MATTERS IS THEY ARE NOT STATIC.
I MAY RETURN TO THE SAME RICH STREAMS OF
INSPIRATION AGAIN AND AGAIN – THE NATURAL
WORLD, EASTERN INFLUENCES OR PRIMITIVE
CULTURES – BUT EACH TIME I DISCOVER
SOMETHING NEW AND FASCINATING. DESIGN
INSPIRATION SHOULD TRANSCEND THE OBVIOUS:
NATURAL IS NOT JUST ABOUT COLLECTING MOSS
WHEN ON A COUNTRY WALK, BUT ABOUT SEEING
SHAPES THAT ARE INTERESTING AND COMPLEX.
GLOBAL IS NOT ABOUT SOUVENIR HUNTING, BUT
ABOUT RECOGNIZING WHAT A RICH VISUAL
SOURCE THE WORLD IS. LUXURY IS NOT ABOUT
HAVING THE FATTEST WALLET, BUT ABOUT
DESIGNING A HOME THAT FITS YOU AS WELL

AS A WARDROBE OF COUTURE CLOTHES WOULD. IT AMAZES ME HOW PEOPLE POUR OVER GLOSSY INTERIOR MAGAZINES AND DESIGN BOOKS FOR INSPIRATION, YET SEEM UNABLE OR UNWILLING TO FORMULATE IDEAS BY OBSERVING WHAT IS AROUND THEM. WHY NOT HAVE FAITH IN YOUR OWN INTUITIVE RESPONSES TO THE WORLD? LEARN TO LOOK NOT JUST WITH YOUR EYES BUT WITH YOUR HEART. THE TRUTH IS THAT STYLE AND TASTE ARE ALL RELATIVE. IT IS NOT A QUESTION OF WHETHER OR NOT SOMEONE HAS GOOD TASTE. IT IS HOW SOMETHING FEELS TO THE INDIVIDUAL. IF THERE IS ONE MESSAGE I WOULD LIKE YOU TO TAKE AWAY FROM THIS SECTION OF THE BOOK, IT IS THIS: OPEN YOUR HEART AND MIND TO THE WORLD, AND FIND THE THINGS THAT CONNECT WITH YOU. HOW ELSE WILL YOU KNOW HOW TO DESIGN YOUR HOME?

Kelly's inspiration

In my office, I have a box file that says "Kelly's – do not touch." Woe to anyone who does, because it is in here that I keep tear sheets, photographs and postcards reminding me of places and images I love. It is one of the pleasures in life, trawling through this file – to which I add constantly – because it is like a memory bank. When I come across a particular image, I am transported back to a certain place at a certain time. It does not just have a visual effect – I can hear it, smell it, taste it, feel it. I start to think not only about the memory, but of how I might translate some of those feelings into my designs. We are all influenced, every single day, by the things we see and experience – the only difference is that I have a more heightened awareness of this than most. I might see a picture of a crisp linen shirt and a woven leather belt, and suddenly I long to create a room that is as crisp and white as that shirt, with nothing to break up the whiteness but a stitched leather headboard. I might walk into the powder room of a restaurant and smell a woman's scent that is so evocative of a certain person that for a while they permeate my thoughts and my designs. Or it might be that when walking in winter I see the dark silhouettes of trees against a white-grey sky and start to think how the starkness of that image might translate into dark wood chairs against linen curtains. The point is that such influences are open to all of us. It is just a question of learning to open not just your eyes but all of your senses.

  Good design connects with people – it is the connection that makes it good. You might open a book of black-and-white photography and see an image that somehow reminds you of something you have experienced – not necessarily a place or a person, but something more subliminal and emotional: happiness, success, celebration. When I am looking through "Kelly's Box," it is not that I am seeking direct inspiration, such as which colors or textures to use, but that I am trying to connect with experiences I have had. That is what I try to bring to my work.

The natural world

AT THE HEART OF MY WORK IS A FEELING OF HARMONY WITH THE NATURAL WORLD. NOT ONLY IS THIS IMPORTANT IN A SPIRITUAL SENSE – TO FEEL AT ONE WITH THE WORLD, IS TO FEEL AT ONE WITH YOURSELF – BUT IT ALSO PROVIDES INSPIRATION ON MANY LEVELS.

Nature is full of the most spectacular colors, textures, forms and patterns, many of which combine contrasting qualities: matte with gloss, light with dark, soft with hard. Think, for example, of the perfect simplicity of lichen on stone, or grass blades etched with frost. Everywhere you look there are striking examples of nature creating beauty, whether shadows on a wheat field as clouds race across the sky, or papery lily pads floating across shimmering water in summer.

The effect of the natural world on my designs can be both direct or subliminal. The first manifests itself through the fact that I like to use natural materials in my work, such as stone, wood, linen, or any of the myriad natural materials available. Flowers are also important to me – so important in fact that they are featured on my design boards alongside upholstery fabric and paint colors. However, I do not limit arrangements to flowers: polished fruit, coral, rope or bark are just as likely to become the focal point of a decorative display.

At a more subliminal level, I take inspiration from what I see around me and interpret it into my own designs. A spiral staircase might, for example, follow the same contours as a sea shell; a satin runner over a wool throw could be a reference to a moonbeam on water; the play between shadow and light in a room may have resulted from watching trees cast long, deep shadows across a lawn.

Finally, the natural world provides something I am passionate about – contrast. My designs are rooted in grids and symmetry – a linear world that provides structure and balance. However, once that is in place, I like to shake it all up by breaking the rigidity with exuberantly asymmetrical forms. The natural world is also a wonderful source of inspiration for craftspeople such as glassmakers and ceramic artists, whose work often provides a sculptural element in my designs.

If there is one thing I would like to open your eyes to it is that natural does not mean rustic. The influences I pick up translate into chic urban interiors just as easily as those situated in unspoiled landscapes. It is a whole new way of seeing.

LEFT This elegant cabinet is one of a pair standing side by side in a dining room; the floating shelves and fiber-optic lighting combine to make the perfect setting for handblown glass, a sculpted plaster shell and a simple glass bowl filled with white sand and coral.

OPPOSITE This spiral staircase of painted cement was custom-built for the apartment; it takes its inspiration from the plaster shell (middle shelf, left) which is displayed in the same room. Its strong architectural form is accentuated by the color white – making it a dynamic focal point.

OPPOSITE Textural contrast and natural materials have been introduced into this marble bathroom by suspending pebbles in resin to create a runner effect down one wall, across the floor and up the opposite wall.

LEFT A pair of cylindrical glass vases filled with dried seedheads creates an artful still life against the plaster-finish wall of this guest bathroom. It is not necessary to buy expensive flowers when beautiful shapes such as these cost so little.

BELOW A woven chair with a wonderfully loose, free-flowing form makes a focal point in an otherwise starkly linear bedroom. In addition, the weave casts interesting shadows where light falls across the stone floor.

Global influences

THE TERM "GLOBAL" HAS BEEN HIGHJACKED IN RECENT YEARS. ALL TOO OFTEN IT IS USED AS A SYNONYM FOR "ETHNIC," A WORD WHICH HAS CEASED TO CELEBRATE CULTURAL DIVERSITY AND COME TO MEAN BUDDHAS, BIRD CAGES AND BAUBLES IN EVERY URBAN HOME.

I raise my hand to being partly responsible for this all-embracing attitude to things Eastern, but what was new and exciting a decade ago is now in danger of looking unimaginative and tired. Global is not something you buy on main street; it is something you travel the world to find. I try to avoid bringing back typical vacation souvenirs; there are few things more depressing than watching a plane load of passengers loading identical rugs, baskets or carved figures into their overhead compartments. And finally, I try not to overdo it – a little can go a very long way indeed.

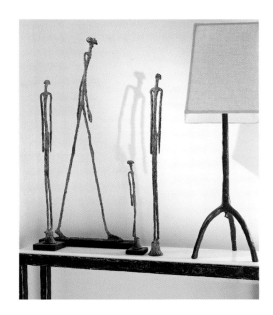

ABOVE Giacometti-style figures from Africa make an interesting composition in this sitting room. The thin iron lamp base and slender bronze console table echo the primitive shapes and metallic finish.

TOP RIGHT Statuesque African drums, each carved from a single piece of wood, make an imposing focal point in this hall. The matte surface of the wood also makes an interesting textural contrast to the glossy floor and the smooth white wall paint.

RIGHT Black-and-white photography of big game animals is another way of introducing African references into the home. Here, the whimsical painted frame softens the stark stone cube of the fireplace surround, as does the row of single-stemmed amaryllis flowers.

Feathered hats – used for ceremonial events by an African tribe – make a striking display against this gargantuan dark chocolate coffee table. Their bold color and effervescent shapes bring a note of drama to the otherwise neutral room.

designing with plants
piet oudolf with noël kingsbury

To me, the term global is subliminal. When I am traveling, I find I mentally step down a notch or two and try to be open to absorbing all sorts of new experiences. It is like filling a virtual filing cabinet in my head with beautiful things – shapes, textures, light, color, pattern, or the juxtaposition of objects. But it is more than visual memory; this filing cabinet can also record feelings, atmospheres and senses. I don't take hundreds of photos or write meticulous notes, I just try to open up a new part in my brain that allows all of this sensory experience to filter in. Back in the office when I begin designing, I find that remembered images will flash into my mind and send me down a certain creative path. In Hawaii, for example, it was the gray of palm tree bark that provided the starting point for a beach house. In New Zealand, it was the feeling of wind on my face that inspired curtains so gossamer light that they would feel like wind stroking the skin. But it might equally be a quality of light or the feeling of walking into a temple that is perfectly calm.

People say the world is getting smaller as flights become less expensive and remote destinations become more accessible. But this is illusion: the world is an enormous place to explore. Everywhere you go there are different ways of speaking, eating, sleeping and living. Do not take this incredible world for granted. Open your eyes to all the beauty it has to offer and find your own way of translating this into your home.

OPPOSITE The perfect order of this Zen-like composition pays homage to Eastern influences, from the simple low bench to the lacquered tray with its row of metal-encased candles and the perfect proportions of dishes and books.

TOP RIGHT A beautifully contoured wooden pedestal provides the ideal place for a glass bowl of greenery, which not only complements the linen Shoji blind, but provides a place for the eye to rest, in keeping with Eastern philosophy.

ABOVE LEFT Japanese-style screens separate this bedroom and bathroom but have been given a contemporary twist by replacing traditional white opaque panels with linen encased in glass for a beautiful translucent effect.

ABOVE RIGHT A stone Buddha provides the centerpiece to this carefully balanced arrangement. Note the subtle link between globe bowls wrapped with rope on one side and the coils of rope within glass bowls on the other side of the built-in shelving.

RIGHT Eastern aesthetics have influenced contemporary furniture in recent years, as with this bronze-and-wood cabinet. The effect has been emphasized by a pair of glass vases filled with coral and an unframed photograph panel that carries the eye into the horizon.

Luxury and detail

LUXURY ONCE MEANT GOLD FIXTURES AND WALL-TO-WALL MARBLE. IT BECAME A DIRTY WORD IN DESIGN, ERASED BY A DESIRE FOR SIMPLICITY AND PURITY. NOW LUXURY HAS TAKEN ON A WHOLE NEW 21ST-CENTURY MEANING.

It is ironic that the luxury goods industry has arguably killed off individuality. The main shopping avenues of the major cities of the world now sport the same names and the same products. Gone are the days when you could travel to New York, Rome or Paris and be excited by the prospect of bringing back a certain special something. No wonder vintage has become such a key word – one-off pieces guarantee originality in a way that luxury brands cannot.

It is true that I love to use luxurious materials in my work, but it would be missing the point to think I use them because they are costly. It is not how expensive they are that is important, but how they feel and what they will bring to a decorative plan. Traditionally luxurious materials such as shagreen, tortoise shell, silver and mother-of-pearl are a part of my palette, but so are humble linen

Luxury is not about the obvious any more – to have a white room filled with the softest fabrics imaginable, such as cashmere, silk or finest quality linen, would be the definition of comfort for many.

OPPOSITE Bathrooms have become the new temples to luxury as materials and fixtures have become increasingly elegant and desirable – the slender faucet, shown here, is a piece of sculpture in its own right, as is the sink carved from one solid piece of dark gray granite.

OPPOSITE, BELOW LEFT A custom-made radiator cover in black glass is a piece that reflects the opulent look of this room. Reflected in it is a sumptuous black goatskin rug and chic chrome furniture.

OPPOSITE, BELOW RIGHT Custom upholstery, such as this voluptuous padded door on a padded wall, has a couture element that makes it really special. A door knob in solid crystal is the only clue to its function.

scrims, gloss paint and Plexiglas. In fact one of the things I love to do is mix the very cheapest with the most luxurious – both are improved by the juxtaposition.

It is also true that I love using natural materials, and sadly some of these are now considered luxuries because they have become scarcer – certain wood and marbles, for example, as well as silks, leathers and semi-precious stones. Similarly, quality craftsmanship has become a form of luxury. The couture houses of Paris struggle to find those who can stitch or embroider to their own impeccably high standards – such people are like gold dust and rightly paid in kind. I too am always searching for gifted artisans who can make my ideas become reality.

The fact is that luxury is another word in urgent need of redefining. Forget gold fixtures, acres of marble and wall-to-wall glitz. The question you have to ask yourself is: what is your luxury? Right now, mine would be a gigantic kitchen, dining room and living area combined, complete with a huge plasma screen TV, where I could do everything and be with everyone in one fabulous space. To me, luxury is also the thought of waking up in the most comfortable bed imaginable and seeing white curtains blowing in the wind. It is a shower that pounds the muscles. It is the patina of a hand-crafted pot. At the turn of the 21st century, I believe luxury is actually about achieving a more relaxed and tailored way of living.

LEFT Mother-of-pearl is one of the most fabulous materials to work with because it has so many shades and so much iridescence caught within its surface – here buttons scattered across a papier-mâché tray make a decorative focal point.

OPPOSITE A black-dyed goatskin rug adds a wonderfully tactile element to this masculine sitting room. Chrome furniture with leather upholstery accentuates the glamorous, almost decadent atmosphere.

Creating theater

ONE OF THE MOST FUN THINGS TO DO AS A DESIGNER IS TO TREAT CERTAIN AREAS OF THE HOME AS A STAGE. IF YOU LOVE A TOUCH OF DRAMA AND SHEER EXTROVERTED WIT, THEN STAND BACK AND LET THE PLAY BEGIN.

When I was a child, I used to love playing with pop-up books – the kind where you could move the characters around on little sticks of cardboard. If taken to the theater, I was always more interested in looking at the stage scenery than following the plot and the acting. I loved watching how the scenery was moved around and changed during the performance. Perhaps then it is no surprise that for me, part of the thrill of designing is thinking about how to get people into a space and how they will feel once they are there.

House design is all about creating "stages" for the way you want to live. They should make you feel your best. However, most of us have a public face and a private one, so this too needs

to be taken into consideration. It might be, for example, that you want a bedroom that is private, meditative and Zen, but you want a dining room and entrance hall that exude glamour. Why not? Just as rooms in the home can be masculine or feminine, so they can be extroverted or introverted. What is important is that they remain true to you.

It is the internal architecture that creates the "stage." Doors that stretch from floor to ceiling, for example, have an imposing effect – as does a panel of glass cut into a ceiling or the sweeping curve of a majestic staircase. It is through skilled joinery that you can transform an ordinary space into an extraordinary one, so work closely with your architect to make your vision become reality.

As with all theater, lighting is key. More than any other ingredient in the design, lighting has the ability to dramatically change the mood of a space. The choice of fabrics is also important because these stamp a signature onto a room – if all the fabrics are grand and expensive, a room will look grand and expensive. That is why I choose to mix the modest with the luxurious and create rooms that are not so easily categorized. In a room where you want to make a statement, add drama through a clever use of color, texture and form. Remember that dining rooms, halls and bathrooms are perfect places for pieces with wow factor because you are in them for relatively short periods of time, and won't tire of the unashamed visual impact.

ABOVE A spectacular stepped ceiling light made of thin plaster tiles creates a fabulous focal point above this circular stairwell. Its exuberant form, like an upside-down wedding cake, is echoed by diamante-adorned chairs and chest-of-drawers in curvy feminine shapes.

OPPOSITE TOP A fabulously oversized bath, carved from a single piece of stone, is as eye-catching as a piece of sculpture in this chic bathroom. By day the skylight above floods it with sunlight; at night it frames the stars.

OPPOSITE BELOW Oak cabinetry inlaid with cane and finished with stitched leather handles is the basis for this striking dressing room. The architectural element is emphasized by subtle lighting and central columns that offer a glimpse through to the room beyond.

Unique focal points

UNIQUE FOCAL POINTS ARE THE VISUAL CENTER OF A ROOM; THE PLACE TO WHICH THE EYE IS DRAWN. THE FOCAL POINT MIGHT BE AN ITEM OF FURNITURE, AN ART PIECE, A LARGE MIRROR OR A REALLY SCULPTURAL LIGHT FIXTURE. THEY ARE NOT THERE TO SIT QUIETLY, BUT TO DEMAND ATTENTION.

ABOVE A traditional crystal chandelier has been encircled in a shiny plastic cylinder for a quirky and unexpected touch in a contemporary kitchen. When lit, the shape of the crystal chandelier can be seen through the laminate like a ghostly outline that is barely there.

RIGHT One-off chairs are like collector's items – choose something with uncompromising form and character such as this green leather-and-chrome chair in a starkly cubist shape. Only one piece is needed to give focus to a room.

As a designer, I use star pieces in two ways. The first is as a starting point to a room design. There are some things that you just see and have to buy, without knowing where they will go. If I see something fabulous that is unlikely to be replicated elsewhere, I snap it up fast. It is fun to begin with an object and build a room around it.

At other times, it is the opposite. I may design a room that is perfect in terms of texture, color, lighting and mood – but it is almost too perfect, too planned. I long to shake the whole thing up in some way, and focal points allow me to do just that. There is a fine line between perfect and bland, so if you ever feel you have slipped from one into the other, start looking for something crazy that will shake up the whole scheme and add a shiver of excitement.

My unique focal points often play visual tricks with scale and proportion. In a small room, such as a bathroom, it can be fun to add something larger than life – such as a huge floor-to-ceiling mirror or a really tall vase. Lights are another fantastic way of playing with scale and form, particularly in a room where you are lying down and it's natural to look up, such as a bedroom or bathroom. But ultimately, it doesn't really matter what your unique focal point is – a piece of sculpture, a one-off chair, a Plexiglas piano – what matters is that you break the rules. The calmer the room you have created appears, the more impact your focal point will have on the end result.

ABOVE An oversized mirror, with silver metallic finish, is a surprising addition to a guest bathroom. In fact using really large objects in very small rooms is a way of making a space appear larger and more important.

LEFT A slender metal wall light, sculpted to resemble a torch, is all that is needed to create interest on this wall. The low bench, with its gentle undulating shape, balances its form by introducing a horizontal line to the vertical one.

Golden rules

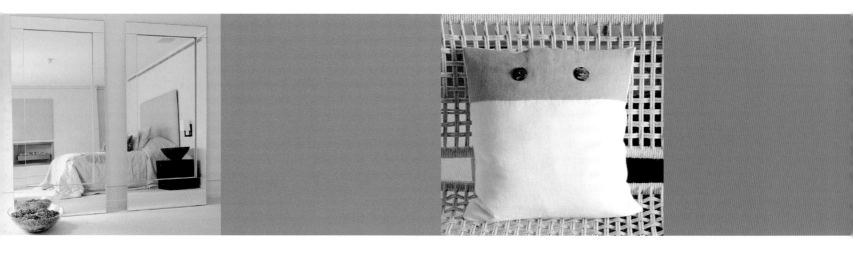

LIVING DINING SLEEPING BATHING

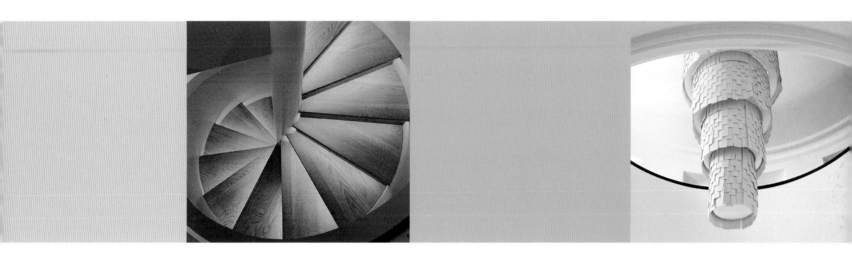

ENTERTAINING WORKING BEING

SUCCESSFUL DESIGN ISN'T ABOUT WHAT PAINT COLORS, FLOORING MATERIALS OR ACCESSORIES YOU CHOOSE. THOSE THINGS ULTIMATELY PLAY A PART, BUT WITHOUT FIRST SOLVING FUNDAMENTAL ISSUES SUCH AS SPATIAL PROBLEMS OR ANALYZING HOW EACH AREA IS TO BE USED, THEY ARE INCONSEQUENTIAL. IF A ROOM IS NOT WELL DESIGNED FROM THE OUTSET, NO AMOUNT OF FABRIC OR EXPENSIVE FURNITURE CAN MAKE IT WORK AS A SUCCESSFUL LIVING SPACE. THIS IS WHAT SEPARATES DESIGNERS FROM DECORATORS. THE LATTER ARE CONCERNED ONLY WITH SURFACE CHANGES WHILE DESIGNERS ARE TRAINED TO GET RIGHT TO THE ROOT OF THE PROBLEM – AND IT IS A FACT THAT EVERY HOUSE OR APARTMENT HAS ITS PROBLEMS. THAT IS WHY THIS CHAPTER IS DEVOTED TO SPACE AND FUNCTION ISSUES. SPACE IS NOT JUST ABOUT HOW MUCH ROOM YOU HAVE,

BUT ABOUT WHETHER YOU CAN IMPROVE IT BY MOVING OR REMOVING INTERNAL WALLS OR BY ADDING PARTITIONS TO CREATE A SERIES OF MORE WORKABLE AREAS. FUNCTION HAS TO DO WITH THE WAY YOU AND YOUR FAMILY LIVE. IT MEANS ANALYZING IN MINUTE DETAIL ALL YOUR DAILY ACTIVITIES AND ROUTINES; FROM WHERE YOU EAT BREAKFAST, TO WHICH SIDE OF THE BED YOU LIKE TO SLEEP ON, TO HOW YOU APPLY MAKEUP. EACH ACTIVITY HAS ITS OWN PATTERN, AND IN ORDER TO CREATE A HOME THAT IS ABSOLUTELY RIGHT FOR YOU, YOU NEED A DESIGN THAT IS IN TUNE WITH THAT ROUTINE. WHETHER YOU ARE USING AN ARCHITECT OR DESIGNER – OR TAKING ON THAT ROLE YOURSELF – THIS CHAPTER SHOULD HELP YOU FOCUS ON CORE DECISIONS CONCERNING SPACE AND FUNCTION THAT ARE THE KEY TO CREATING A SUCCESSFUL AND HARMONIOUS LIVING SPACE.

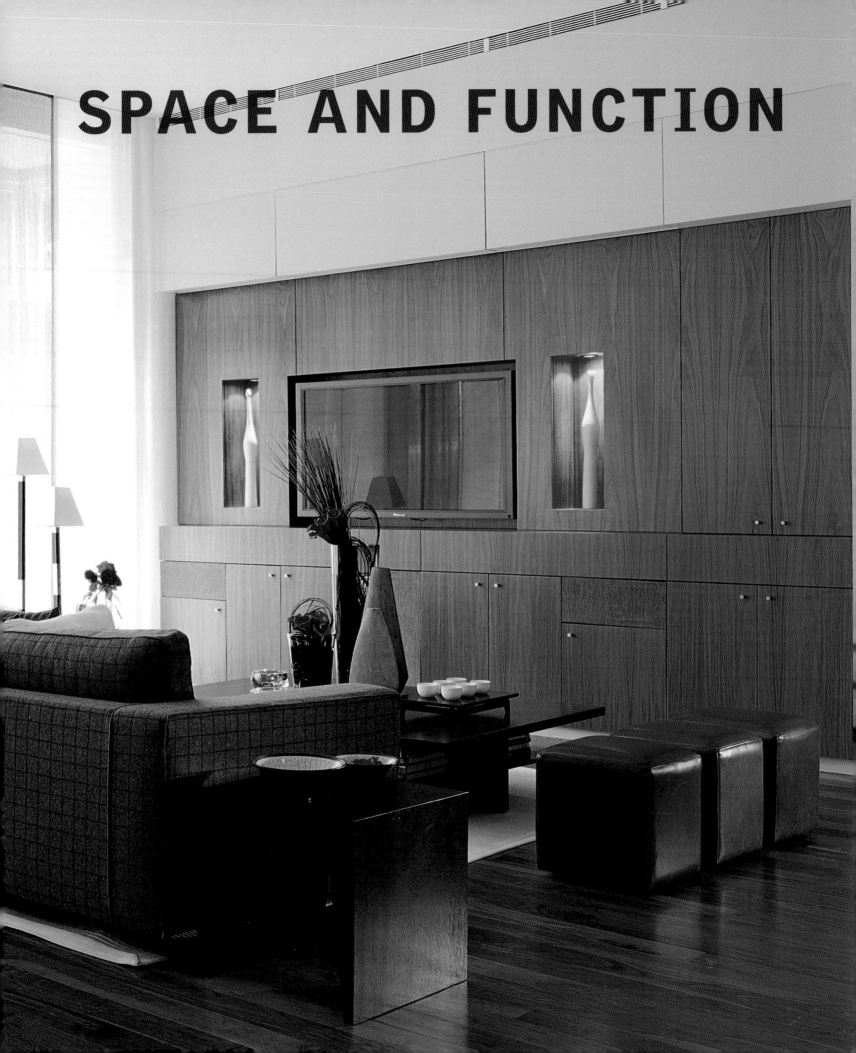

SPACE AND FUNCTION

Analyzing space

DO NOT BE DAUNTED BY THE THOUGHT OF DESIGNING A SPACE. ALTHOUGH IT HELPS TO HAVE AN UNDERSTANDING OF FLOOR PLANS AND ELEVATIONS, A LOT COMES DOWN TO COMMON SENSE, AN AWARENESS OF HOW YOU LIKE TO LIVE.

The first step is deciding how you are going to use the space at your disposal. The configuration of rooms is a direct response to function. In simple terms you will know how many bedrooms and bathrooms you require, for example, but are there other rooms on your wish list? It may be you long for a wine cellar, a dressing room, a home gym or a separate suite for the nanny. Writing your wish list should be the first step. You may not be able to afford it in terms of money and space, but it is always better to start with the big picture and work backwards. Often people are surprised at what can be created by making a few simple structural changes and employing the skill of lateral thinking.

A blueprint is useful at this stage. By having a complete picture of the space available you will see how rooms may work in a totally different layout, by way of knocking through, dividing up or extending. You may change your mind from day to day, but keep the plan accessible and play around with different solutions until you really can visualize the end result. The core transformation of an interior takes place at blueprint stage.

Budget is the next consideration. Nobody likes to address the question of money directly, because we would all prefer to pretend we are richer than we are. However, it is important to be realistic. The fact is you will spend every penny you have and everything will cost twice as much as you expected. Create a budget on that basis. The good news is that not everything will have to be paid for upfront. If you are employing an architect or master builder, ask them to draw up a building schedule clearly showing at which points you will have to spend money and how much.

If you are working with an architect or designer, he or she will probably draw up elevations for every room. These help you understand the vertical space as well as the horizontal one – an

GOLDEN RULES: SPATIAL ELEMENTS

1 Curved glass panels set into the upper walls of this dramatic round entrance hall open up the space even further. The wood frames also make a visual link to the black lacquered floor below.

2 Extravagant white curtains cascading to the floor emphasize the proportions of the window, the curve of the stairs and the theatricality of such a bold space.

3 Architectural elements have been accentuated by the use of both convex and concave curved stairs in different scales, linked by graphic black and white.

4 Black lacquered parquet flooring makes a dramatic runner across the white marble floor – the contemporary version of the red carpet leading visitors to the rooms beyond.

5 A boldly sculptural ceiling light made of thin plaster tiles draws the eye, making a link between upstairs and downstairs. Coordinating wall lights echo its striking effect.

OPPOSITE This magnificent hall has a touch of original Hollywood glamour from the black glossiness of the floor to the billowing white curtains and theatrically curved staircase. Oversized furniture, lighting and large African drums help to accentuate the impression.

elevation will show structural elements such as radiators, doors and windows, and also decorative items such as curtains, wall lights, furniture height and so on. In a sense the elevation allows you to feel as though you are walking around a virtual version of the space. It also helps you avoid mistakes such as buying armchairs with arms that will not fit under the dining table, or building in drawers that will bang the bedside table when opened. Blueprints and elevations should always be drawn to the same scale to avoid confusion. Draw furniture outlines to this scale as well and you can physically place it on the plans to find the best arrangement.

Designing a house should be like buying couture. It allows you to think about your way of doing things, from how you put your makeup on, to what you like to cook. Plans might seem boring, but in fact they are the tool by which you can make your dream home become reality. Once you have solved the problems of function and space, you can begin to think about each individual area. Gather tear sheets, brochures and any other visual references and start by putting these into folders, one for every room. Bedrooms with en suite bathrooms or dressing rooms can be kept together, since the design between closely related spaces is important.

As you whittle down your choices, you will be left with references for everything from home furnishings and lighting to technology and art. It is crucial to consider every element of the room in association with everything else if you are going to create a space that is both workable and beautiful.

GOLDEN RULES: DRAWINGS AND BLUEPRINTS

☆ Make sure that every blueprint and drawing that you come up with follows the same scale so that you can compare like with like and avoid confusion.

☆ These must always be dated so that you - and everyone else involved - know which is the most current version.

☆ Take your time. The leap between reading blueprints and being able to visualize the finished space is a big one.

☆ Vertical space is as important as horizontal space, so use elevations in conjunction with the blueprint for a three-dimensional view.

☆ Learn to use a slide rule so you can draw furniture outlines to scale and work out where everything should be placed.

TOP LEFT It is a convention that fireplaces are usually placed centrally on walls, but in this indulgent bedroom, it has been moved to the left, becoming more of a decorative feature. The flat screen television, set into custom-made wood panels, now takes center stage.

OPPOSITE The double height of this living room has been accentuated by custom shelving and floor-to-ceiling parachute silk curtains. An atrium allows the upper space to be used, while keeping the whole area as open as possible.

LIVING rooms are the engine house of the home. They have to reflect the public you, while also allowing the private you to relax. They need to provide comfortable seating for many different activities, from watching television to chatting with friends over a glass of wine. And the chances are they will be used equally by every member of the household, and so have to be flexible enough to accommodate all the family's needs.

The place to start is seating. Buying a sofa or armchair is like buying a bed – only the best will do for a piece of furniture that is going to be used on such a regular basis. Floor plans are useful when designing any room, but when planning out the living room space they are vital. How else will you know how big a sofa or coffee table to buy? Remember that the plan must show both negative and positive space: the first is the space taken up by furniture; the second is the leftover space around the furniture that allows free traffic and uninterrupted access around the room. Drawing up a floor plan also helps you to visualize how the room will be used and where furniture should be placed. When arranging the room, try to avoid having all the seats facing the television. L-shaped or U-shaped arrangements work well and can lead the eye to a focal point, such as a fireplace.

When it comes to deciding whether you want to display or conceal technology such as the television, that is a personal choice. I would come down in favor of display because this is the 21st century and I prefer to live in today, rather than in the past. However, that does not mean that TVs, DVDs or surround-sound systems have to dominate the room. Custom-built shelves or cabinets should allow them to merge quietly into the background, as will flat display screens.

The living room is a place where it is important to have attractive objects throughout that draw the eye. There should be something to see from every seat, whether an artful arrangement on the adjacent table, thoughtfully dressed shelves or a collection of art. Remember you are striving not only for physical comfort but visual comfort too.

ABOVE LEFT This harmonious living room is a calm, quiet blend of whites and taupes, complemented by sepia-tinted photographs. Balance is important, as shown by the row of ceramic bowls on the table and the positioning of pillows.

ABOVE RIGHT This grand living room has two areas – shown here is the television sitting area – whereas the main section of the room (shown opposite) is for entertaining. Perfect symmetry emphasizes its somewhat formal atmosphere.

RIGHT In the other section of the living room, double doors open into the hall. Comfortable seating is a priority in a room designed for guests; art glass and organically shaped bronze tables accentuate its opulence.

In a light, spacious dining room, linen curtains and sleek, modern chairs emphasize the feeling of openness. Shoji panels are a clever way of introducing runners to walls and make an interesting textural link to the other fabrics in the room.

DINING

rooms are used less frequently than other areas of the home and are reserved for special events, so they offer the chance to create something really dramatic. Remember that these are usually nighttime rooms, so atmospheric lighting is key. This should include not only carefully positioned downlighters to wash the walls with light, but unique focal points such as antique chandeliers wrapped in Plexiglas, or fiber optics set into the glass surface of a table. They are also rooms perfect for displaying collections – particularly decorative ones such as handblown glass, carved wood or black-and-white photographs.

However, many people prefer to eat in the kitchen rather than in a dedicated dining room. Kitchen dining is less formal, more fun – and therefore more in tune with modern living. Assuming there is enough space, the ideal is to zone the kitchen into three distinct areas – cooking, dining and living.

You can use different textures to mark out the perimeters of each zone. Start with the floor. If you choose stone for the kitchen floor, for example, you may prefer to lay wood or leather where the dining table will go. Lighting is another useful tool. Whereas kitchen lighting needs to be sharp and directional, in order to make food preparation and cooking safe, dining lighting should be soft and atmospheric. I often use spotlights in the kitchen, but then hang pendant lights very low over the table. This creates an atmosphere of intimacy, quite different from the surrounding area. Here, the style of the dining-room furniture should be sympathetic to the kitchen design, but also different from it to make the finished effect more interesting.

KITCHENS

are so much more than a place to cook – they are a place to sit and talk with family and friends. Some people really love to cook – and therefore they need a cook's kitchen – but many of us are more likely to use ours as the social center of the household. Be honest: is this a kitchen for preparing lavish meals, or in which you want to snack and chat?

When budgeting for a kitchen, remember that they can cost double the initial quote when you take all the appliances, accessories and decorative details into account. They also turn your world upside down while being installed, so you don't want to repeat the experience too quickly. It makes sense therefore to deal with a custom kitchen company, rather than trying to oversee it all yourself. Put two days aside to visit the kitchen showrooms and talk to designers about your needs. Really think first about how much you cook, what you cook and when you cook. A good kitchen company will not only come up with a design that looks sensational but also takes into account your own method of working.

If you are like me and cooking is low on your list of priorities, what you really want is a show kitchen: one that looks as fabulous as the rest of the house. My own is white lacquer – I have had it a few years, but I still absolutely love it. I am not so keen on the trend for stainless steel or aluminium kitchens. They were created for hygiene and are very cold. Personally, I prefer dark woods, bamboo or glass.

Cooks' kitchens are driven by function, so work surfaces, for example, have to be practical, hygienic and durable. Granite is best, but I recommend using the reverse side, which has a dull finish and is often far more attractive. Marble is great for pastry-making, but it stains if not maintained carefully. However, this may not matter. Like a leather floor, it can look better as it acquires a less pristine appearance. In a show kitchen where you don't have to consider practicalities, you can go for something with real wow factor, such as thick concrete slabs with cutouts for the sink, or a glass backsplash lit with fiber optics from behind.

The floor should provide textural and visual interest. Consider materials such as wood, terrazzo or poured plaster – even poured concrete can look fabulous, particularly with stone set into it.

ABOVE Two island units were created in this spacious kitchen: the one to the left is a place to eat; the one to the right is for the preparation of food. The symmetrical arrangement is emphasized by the runner effect on the floor.

ABOVE Dark wood and a lack of natural light could combine to make this city kitchen feel oppressive, but this has been avoided by adding a panel of glass to the wall through which adjacent spaces can be glimpsed.

LEFT The use of an accent color, such as the red shown here, is a great way of breaking up rich woods and hard lines in the kitchen. A small island unit with bar stools adds a note of informality and relaxation.

OPPOSITE BELOW White is a perennially popular choice for kitchens. Solid doors would look too claustrophobic in this relatively modest space so semi-tranluscent ones have been chosen instead. Metal lights floating in glass accentuate the feeling of lightness.

TOP LEFT A softly upholstered swivel chair and floating sculptural light create a quiet reading area in a corner of this peaceful bedroom. A square of canvas above the fireplace mirrors the geometric shape of the lampshade.

BELOW LEFT A dramatically oversized upholstered headboard has been used to emphasize the height of this magnificent bedroom suite, which takes up one floor of the house and includes both a sitting and study area.

ABOVE The concrete platform that doubles as bed base in this simple Zen bedroom is wide enough that bedside tables are unnecessary. Wall-mounted lamps are an acceptable alternative to conventional bedroom lamps.

OPPOSITE This low-level bed draws attention to the height of the room and the shapes of the eaves above. On each of the floating bedside tables are miniature compositions of carefully placed dishes and vases, with photographs above.

BEDROOMS are often treated as second best in a house, perhaps because people

think they do not matter as much as rooms that are on public display. But ask yourself this: shouldn't you value your rest and relaxation? Don't you deserve the very best?

To my mind, the bedroom should be everything you dream of – sensual, luxurious, indulgent and heart-stoppingly beautiful. This is a room that will affect how well you sleep at night and what mood you wake up in. Surely nothing could be more important than that.

Designing your own bedroom gives you the perfect opportunity to express your personality, so don't hold back. Visually, I think that the style of your bedroom should link with the other rooms in the house, but somehow be even more you in spirit.

Just as a kitchen no longer functions solely as a room for cooking in, so a bedroom is not only for sleeping. Think about everything you like to do in your bedroom from watching TV or practicing yoga to making love and cuddling your children. When it comes to design, this room must function practically for every activity that goes on here; it also needs to reflect changing moods. Good lighting and curtains or blinds are obviously a crucial element in this room. Not only do they allow you to alter the atmosphere – often at the flick of a switch – but they are something you see when lying down. In bedrooms and also bathrooms, it is pivotal to have lighting that is both functional and pleasing to the eye from all angles and viewpoints.

BATHROOM

BATHROOM design needs to be carefully thought through because it is not something you can change easily. Once the plumbing is installed and the bath and floor positioned, it is costly to alter. It is also complex in terms of function: after all, this is a room where you may want a quick, refreshing shower in the morning, and where you want to bathe and relax at night. It also needs a lot of storage space – not just for bulky items such as towels, but for small ones such as contact lenses. If a bathroom is to work successfully, you have to work out in advance exactly what you will do here and take into account where everything will be kept. If you want to create a totally couture bathroom, then commission a craftsman to make cabinets that will include a customized space for every item from lipsticks to toilet paper.

The bath is the unique focal point; think of it as a piece of sculpture that should be set center stage. Contrast is always the key. If you like old-fashioned clawfoot designs, then use one in a very contemporary setting. A good power shower is a feature of most modern bathrooms, but with this item function counts more than aesthetics.

Because the bathroom is full of hard, clean surfaces, you must find ways of softening its appearance. Lighting is one way of doing this – have a mix of directional task lighting and easily dimmed mood lighting. My own bath is raised on stilts Japanese-style with lighting that floods the floor below. At night I light scented candles and turn all the other bathroom lights off, so that I can float in the darkness with just a pool of light around the bath. Upholstered furniture will also take the sharpness off the hard lines of a bathroom. If you have the space, a towelling bench is ideal. If not, find room for a bathroom chair upholstered in soft linen or fine silk.

LEFT For a large bathroom, buy the most beautiful bath you can and place it centrally to create a piece of sculpture. Here the spa-like setting has been added to with glass globes of simple fresh flowers and creamy porcelain vases.

BELOW The same bathroom as left: custom-made cabinetry has been commissioned to create a double washbasin with centrally placed television that can be seen from the bath. The Buddha above adds an Eastern touch.

TOP ROW LEFT Ceramic bowls on a wooden countertop are the contemporary versions of traditional washstands - a move away from the built-in approach popular a few years ago. Taps set into the stone surround add an elegant touch.

TOP ROW CENTER The shelf-like contours of this wooden basin might not appear practical, but in fact water gathers and drains away easily. A slender glass screen protects the floor, while the flat ends are perfect for storing toiletries.

TOP ROW RIGHT A glass basin on a stone pedestal, with chic chrome faucets and wenge cabinets, provides a wonderful textural contrast in this elegant bathroom. The shelves are usually hidden behind invisible sliding doors.

OPPOSITE, MIDDLE ROW FAR LEFT This freestanding basin unit in a bedroom is the link between that and the en suite bathroom. The Murano-style glass vase and a horizontal strip of mirror add decorative touches to this transitional area.

OPPOSITE, MIDDLE ROW LEFT White bathrooms are classic; this semi-suspended basin adds a contemporary feel. Introduce modern accessories such as rows of identical pots or single stem roses in bowls of white sand.

OPPOSITE, BELOW LEFT Sliding glass doors conceal shelves of white towels in this starkly elegant shower room. The stone wall and stone shower enclosure provide textural contrast to opaque glass and fittings of chrome.

ABOVE Reminiscent of a Turkish bath, this one has been carved into stone set at floor height so you step down into it. Eastern influences continue with paneled walls and low benches that have both a functional and decorative use.

LEFT Rows of identical objects are the perfect way of dressing this Zen-inspired bathroom. Note the use of different scales from tiny pots along the bath edge to larger ceramic bowls and practical floor-standing baskets.

POWDER ROOMS offer

an opportunity to push the design boundaries. This is partly because they are small rooms, so whatever you do here will not have an overwhelming impact; partly it is because no one will spend too long here, so you can be a little bolder.

However, bold does not mean gimmicky. It does mean you can break some rules. For example, mixing colors of tubs and sinks in a bathroom does not work. A white bathtub with a black sink, for example, is jarring. The effect is messy, rather than chic.

In a powder room you could have a white toilet and a black sink, and they could live happily together. It's difficult to explain why this should be the case, but it has to do with scale and mood. A bathroom should be a place to relax. A powder room, on the other hand, can be a bit edgy.

Look for unexpected treatments of conventional things. A mirror, for example, is a must-have in most powder rooms. However, rather than hang one over the sink, why not take strips of mirror and hang them in horizontal bands around the room?

Because these rooms are small spaces, they also allow you to indulge in luxurious materials that would usually be prohibitively expensive in a large bathroom. The same goes for hand-crafted plaster finishes on the walls or fabric at the window. Finally, remember that in a small room it is important to use a large scale object – a truly dramatic ceiling light might be the perfect ingredient to bring a sense of importance to the smallest of rooms.

TOP ROW LEFT The focus here is on the textured resin floor above which the toilet appears to float. The wood paneled wall is in fact a series of concealed "push-release" cupboards, which provide useful storage for toiletries and towels.

TOP ROW CENTER A stone basin sits on a simple wenge cabinet, which provides ample space for toiletries and display. Units such as this were once exclusive, but are now readily available from bathroom stores.

TOP ROW RIGHT This specially commissioned bench toilet seat in stained wood adds a touch of wit to a very contemporary apartment. Black floor and white walls emphasize the starkly geometric effect of rectangles and circles.

ABOVE LEFT Accent color, such as these red tiles, has been used to add interest to a teenager's bathroom. The cutout shape of the wash basin, integrated panel of mirror and curve of the faucet accentuate the architectural form of the room.

ABOVE RIGHT A floating glass basin is the centerpiece of this guest bathroom. Faucets are integrated into the stone backdrop so they do not interfere with the effect, while a perfectly proportioned mirror finishes the look perfectly.

OPPOSITE A white ceramic sink on a wooden pedestal sets the tone for this elegant room. The shelf above is the perfect display area for greenery in glass boxes, mirrored by a line of practical black storage canisters below.

HOME OFFICES

HOME OFFICES reflect one of the biggest changes to interior design over the last 15 years – our dependence on technology. Once there were hi-fi's, televisions and video recorders; now there are DVDs, surround-sound systems, home computers, faxes and printers - not just one per home but multiplied from room to room. Not only that, but our homes are increasingly protected by high-tech security systems, which also add to the now ubiquitous list of technological devices.

For a long time, people tried to conceal technology but I generally leave TV and computer screens exposed, but hide ugly hard drives, printers, DVDs and all the other metal boxes that make up modern entertainment systems within custom-made cabinetry. Until comparatively recently, wires were also an unsightly problem. However, now it is easy to have everything integrated into a single cable; wireless technology also promises great things for the future.

Many of us now do either some or all of our work from home, and too often the home office is as bland and unimaginative as the conventional type. A better solution is to create a space that can function both as an office and as a recreational room. My own is the place where I read, call friends on the phone, use my computer and deal with correspondence. It is a home office with the emphasis firmly on home rather than on office.

A home office doesn't have to be located in a dedicated room such as the smallest bedroom. In fact dining rooms are often the perfect location because most people eat in the kitchen and so dining rooms become underused spaces within the house. This dual function also prevents a more formal dining area from becoming a neglected place that is rarely used. A bare dining-room table looks rather sad and uninspiring; one covered with books opened at relevant pages, looks vibrant and interesting. All it requires is a place for storage – bookcases are ideal – where everything can be put away when you want to entertain here.

Another reason for having a room that doubles as a work space is that books themselves bring so much to a room. Compared to sculpture or paintings, they are very inexpensive yet add a whole new layer of character and interest. A collection or a display of some kind is an asset here because not only will it divert attention away from technology, but give the eye somewhere to rest. There is no reason why a work space should be devoid of beauty.

ABOVE Work spaces within the home can be very sparse – the focus in this study is a simple table for computer and printer. The Plexiglas chair is nearly invisible against the light coming through the Shoji blinds.

LEFT Comfort was the priority in this room for reading and relaxation. Sumptuously upholstered chairs have been placed in front of the plasma screen. Cabinetry is used to hide other home electronics, and to display decorative glass that frames the flat television screen.

OPPOSITE The secret of integrating technology into the home is to display computer screens, which are often an attractive design element, and to conceal unsightly wires and cords. Here the work space has been softened with a decorative display.

HALLWAYS are your calling

card to the world. If you were meeting someone for the first time, the chances are you would like to look your best. The same rule applies to the hall; as soon as visitors enter the house they will start to get an impression of your style, your taste, you, depending on what they see.

The surprising thing is that the hall is often treated as a second-class citizen, with just the minimum amount of money spent on its design and decoration. This is a shame on two fronts: one, because it will fail to make a good impression; two, because in relation to the rest of the house it is a fairly small area and doesn't need to cost an arm and a leg to do well. If you have fallen in love with a floor that you could not afford to put into your living room, why not consider using it in the hall? Similarly, most halls have only one window – so dress it in the most fabulous and luxurious textures.

You should also think about the different viewpoints in the hall space. The most important is the entrance from which you see it for the first time, but the hall includes many doors and from each one there should be a pleasant view. Do not ignore how it looks from the top of the stairs as well. Halls are the perfect place for one really striking central light because you can enjoy the way it looks from both above and below. Finally, in a small hall, think about larger doors for added effect. This will make the space appear bigger and create a sense of grandeur in a modest-sized space.

ABOVE Architectural elements are integral to the success of the hall. Here doors have been taken right up to the ceiling to create a more imposing atmosphere. Discreet spotlights – set at foot level – lead the eye up the stairs.

LEFT When working with original features, such as these elaborate banisters, keep colors muted. The focal point here is the stairwell window where sheer curtains have been designed to fall in pools on the floor.

TOP RIGHT Wood-and-stone stairs have been designed to look as though they are floating through space, emphasizing the airy atmosphere of this light-filled house. The glass banister provides safety without spoiling the effect.

The same hall as top right, page 56:
the materials chosen by the
architects – wood and stone – are a
way of linking the different spaces
of the house. Custom cabinetry, such
as the integrated fish tank, is key to
the unified effect.

A floating shelf replaces the traditional console in this period hall. A row of test tube vases with single stem roses creates an installation, which is further complemented by black-and-white photography of flowers above.

opposite These statuesque lights were specially made for this Japanese-inspired hall; the padded wall and architectural woodwork are also key features. Traditional Eastern chairs have been lacquered and dressed with white vinyl pillows.

ABOVE LEFT The floor of this balcony is a mix of decking and glass – the latter designed to flood the rooms below with light. Furniture, rather than plants, is the focus of this space – positioned to look out over the perfectly manicured garden.

ABOVE RIGHT Topiarized hornbeam trees create the grid of this perfectly balanced garden, complemented by cubes of yew and tightly clipped boxwood hedging. The shadows they make add an additional layer of interest to the form and proportion created.

FAR LEFT Mounds of synthetic grass complemented by black stone and white gravel create an installation reminiscent of a Japanese-style garden. The roof on which they sit could not support a conventional garden, but this is a clever substitute.

FAR RIGHT A line of galvanized plant holders provide privacy for this roadside balcony, while also creating a harmonious effect. Topiaries, such as boxwood are architecturally desirable because they provide color and form all-year round.

OUTDOOR SPACES and roof gardens should

never be designed as an afterthought to the interior, but in tandem. After all, each space has a direct relation to the other. When you are inside looking out, you don't want to feel that the design stops and then starts again in a new form. You want a sense of unity. Similarly, when you are outside, you want to feel that you are bridging the gap between the interior of your home and the world beyond.

But first there are hard-core design decisions to tackle, concerning the installation of electrical wiring and plumbing. First consider at what times of the day, week and year, the terrace will be most used. Is it where you plan to breakfast, or are more likely to use in the evening? External lighting is central to the design concept if you are going to gain maximum use from it. You might also want to invest in a patio heater, so that chilly night air does not drive you and your guests inside too early. An irrigation system is essential if you are not always going to be at home to water the plants. In the first three years, it will be your garden's life-support system.

When planning your terrace, study how the sun moves and the changing effect of the light. How can you best capitalize on this? Repetition of materials can also be effective – in fact the best garden designs are intrinsically simple. Use evergreen plants where possible, because they provide all-year shape and interest. I love flowers in the home but not in the garden – the visual pleasure they give is too fleeting. When choosing plants, you must be able to visualize how they will change over time in terms of height and density.

Just as I use a grid system when designing interiors, so I like to see trees and plants positioned on an underlying grid structure. There is something satisfying about the contrast between the sharp lines of the design and the soft organic shapes of the plants themselves. Objects such as planters, urns and stone balls can also be placed in lines to emphasize the structure of the design. Always use an odd number of garden objects to avoid too much symmetry. Water features are also desirable because they bring in texture and sound, while creating another layer of light and shadow.

Mood

BEFORE DECORATING A ROOM, DECIDE ON THE MOOD
YOU WOULD LIKE TO CREATE AND HOW YOU WOULD
LIKE IT TO FEEL – RELAXED OR ENERGIZED, CALM OR
STIMULATED, EXTROVERTED OR CONTEMPLATIVE.

It is a good idea to form an idea of the sort of mood you want to create and how it relates to the room's function before making any major decorative decisions. Different states of mind can be fostered through the use of color, texture, form and lighting. In fact it is possible to radically change the entire mood of a room to suit the occasion by simply manipulating color and lighting. Dining rooms are good examples of places that often benefit from a different atmosphere by day – when they are more likely to be used for family meals or informal lunches – than by their nighttime, supper party one.

However, unless you live in a large house or apartment, the chances are that you need most rooms to be dual functional. Many people now work at least some of the time at home but don't necessarily have dedicated home offices. It may be that you use an area within the living, dining or bedroom as a work zone. During the day, it is important that this space makes you feel efficient and ordered. But when you want to switch off, you must to be able to change the mood to a more tranquil, restful one. The same goes for your bedroom and bathroom: in the morning they need to make you feel refreshed and energetic, and ready to face the challenges of the day ahead, but at night they should engender a feeling of relaxation and harmony.

ABOVE AND OPPOSITE The same dining room shown by day and night. The evening room uses a variety of light sources from the sculptural ceiling lights and contemporary standard lamp to the fiber optics beneath the shelves, subtle ceiling spotlights and the free-standing candelabra. The final layer of light is the candles in the glass storm lanterns along the central runner. The whole mood is sensual and intimate. It looks quite different by day but is kept dressed to retain interest. Bare tables and unused dining rooms look pretty sad and neglected.

BELOW LEFT This outside sitting area is covered and has protection from the weather but looks directly onto the garden beyond. Wicker furniture and white linen covers create a relaxed laid-back mood. Lamp shades are also linen.

BELOW RIGHT Fires create an immediate feeling of coziness and comfort. Here soft upholstery and thickly banded cushions accentuate the warmth. A contemporary reading light, positioned by the chair, adds to the intimate mood at night.

Scale

USING OBJECTS OF DIFFERENT SIZES ALLOWS YOU TO INJECT A ROOM WITH CHARACTER AND WIT. IF EVERYTHING IS OF THE SAME PROPORTION, THE RESULT CAN BE UNINSPIRED AND PREDICTABLE. OVER- AND UNDER-SCALING IS A DECORATING MASTERSTROKE THAT HAS BEEN AROUND FOR CENTURIES.

Scale is one of the most difficult things to learn to use effectively in design, but it can make more difference to the overall effect than color, texture or display.

Rooms where everything is of the same size are predictable and bland. There is nothing for the eye to rest on naturally. It is as if every decorative ingredient merges into the next. In contrast, think about how our ancestors used scale to impart grandeur and importance to certain buildings – there is nothing bland about the soaring arches of a Gothic cathedral or the imposing outline of the Empire State Building. Statues, paintings, carpets and lights were very often commissioned to fit vast spaces that were much grander in scale than their human occupants. They understood not only that large rooms needed large objects, but that large objects could make even modest rooms appear larger.

In fact overscaling has been an essential of the decorator's bag of tricks for centuries. It might no longer be about large tapestries or tall columns, but it can be interpreted in other ways. Think of floors made with huge stone slabs and great planks of wood. Imagine doors that stand from the floor right up to the ceiling or a block of fabric Shoji panels used to divide rooms. Consider the impact of unique focal points of furniture such as sculptural chandeliers, massive urns or gargantuan mirrors propped against walls. When it comes to big scale, the rule is simple: find the biggest the room will take. As a rule of thumb, this will stand you in good stead for sofas, beds, tables, cabinetry and doors.

GOLDEN RULES: SCALE

1 Scale is an effective way of introducing drama into a space. These huge wooden pots from Africa make a bold statement as you enter this drawing room. Height is a key element in this interior design and they set the tone for that immediately.

2 Extra-tall reading lights at each side of the room also stress the vertical lines. Note too how their geometric shape is echoed by the black frames around the photography, hung at each side of the fireplace rather than over it.

3 Height is again accentuated by over-sized glass cylinders filled with snake grass – another symmetrical element in the room's composition. It is as though every ingredient in the room is pulling the eye upwards.

4 In contrast the low Japanese-style bench introduces a horizontal line into the grid, but without crossing the line of vision as you walk into the room. Carefully placed pillows of different sizes link to the vertical once more.

However, in order to show contrast of scale you always need to balance out a room containing a few carefully chosen large objects with smaller scale ones. That means understanding how to use small objects. In some ways, this is even harder than using large pieces – the worst thing you could do is create a tablescape of itsy-bitsy, unrelated objects. So if in doubt, follow a few simple rules: choose small-scale objects for form and textural contrast; replicate them in rows or groups; do not use too many or mix in much else; and position them adjacent to large-scale objects for added impact. So, for example, you might have an enormous door with a line of small black-and-white photographs hung along each side. Or you could have a classically grand black marble fireplace on which stand three miniature silver bowls. Or perhaps, a single stem rose displayed against a backdrop of super-enlarged images of roseheads. The idea is to create an energy between objects of different scales, but also to use the contrast of scale to keep an overall sense of balance and interest in the room.

Remember too that size is a way of emphasizing the underlying grid structure of a room, which I consider essential in terms of design. Oversized objects can lead the eye along vertical or horizontal lines. So, for example a low table which is extra wide might be placed close to a very tall lamp. Small objects which echo the grid structure can then be situated nearby for extra definition.

GOLDEN RULES: USING SCALE

☆ In a large room, you need large-scale objects that fill the space and make it appear more intimate. The rule is: buy the biggest you can.

☆ In small rooms, introduce a few overscaled objects because they will trick the eye into believing the space is bigger than it is.

☆ The important thing is not to have every element of the same size: mix in large with small rather than opting for medium.

☆ Small-scale objects will make a modest-sized room appear small but have the effect of making large rooms appear huge.

☆ When using objects of different sizes in the same room, there should be a textural or color link that unites them.

ABOVE In a spacious living room, large objects such as the double width coffee table and generous-sized sofas emphasize the space. In contrast, small ceramic bowls and tiny pillows play on the use of small scale in big rooms.

LEFT Accessories have been used here to draw the eye away from the centrally placed television. Tall glass vases filled with papyrus accentuate the grid formed by the horizontal cabinet. The wooden sculpture to the left mirrors their effect.

OPPOSITE TOP In a large dressing room, a huge mirror propped against the wall and a tall lamp are both practical and striking. Note how floor-to-ceiling closets are fitted with long handles to exaggerate their height.

OPPOSITE BELOW A row of wooden orchid planters is cleverly used to create impact in a dining room with little floor space. Their shape is echoed by cylindrical glass ceiling lights and simple glass candle holders on the dining-room table.

Symmetry and balance

IF A ROOM IS NOT SYMMETRICAL, YOU HAVE TWO CHOICES: TO TRY AND FOOL
THE EYE INTO THINKING THE ROOM IS MORE BALANCED THAN IT IS, OR TO
ACCEPT THAT IT IS OFF-KEY AND CONCENTRATE ON GIVING IT FOCUS INSTEAD.

GOLDEN RULES: SYMMETRY

1 Symmetry and order are essential in the bedroom if you are going to sleep well. Even if you don't have a perfectly proportioned room, try to find the center point and from this work out the best position for the bed. Emphasize balance by creating an interior that looks like a mirror image – here curtains, chairs, pictures, tables, and lamps have their identical counterpart on the other side of the room.

2 Make use of vertical lines – these are like an upright skeletal structure where rooms are concerned. See how they are used here on the curtains, headboard and double-hung photograph frames to make the room stand tall. Horizontal lines on the voile under-curtains and landscape photographs provide balance.

3 Furniture doesn't have to be placed at the end of the bed. These sculptural chairs stand in their own space, drawing the eye into the room and focusing it on the bed beyond. Useful at night for books or clothes, their main role is to add energy and dynamism to the room through their curved shape. The rule here is "Don't follow convention."

4 In order for a symmetrical room to work well, there must also be asymmetry. The three vases of pale pink roses to the left of the bed are all that is needed to create another layer of interest. The way they are positioned in successive heights also contributes to the room's composition. Look to the bedside table on the right and you will see a row of single stem blooms that echo their presence.

5 The photograph hung above the headboard is the focal point for the whole room. It balances beautifully with the width of the bed and is perfectly central, providing an anchor to the rest of the room. Note how the bed is symmetrically arranged, other than the one pillow propped to interrupt the central line. This is intentional: create symmetry and then gently break it.

Naturally, a symmetrical room is always the best possible start. If I am lucky enough to begin with an architecturally harmonious space then I seek to retain it through every element of the design. However, many rooms are not naturally symmetrical and may be too difficult or too costly to alter structurally. Instead you can improve proportions by rectifying some of the room's faults through clever cabinetry, such as building in shelves where there are niches, or building a wall of cupboards so that an adjacent window appears to be more central than it actually is. The way a room is lit or furniture is positioned can also help trick the eye into believing the space is more harmonious than it is.

The second approach involves "throwing" the eye onto certain areas within the room by using "over-scale." In doing so, you draw the attention away from other more awkward spaces. This works best if you keep the design neutral and quiet. Remember too that asymmetry can be an effective way of creating dymanic tension in a room – just as different scales and textures produce stimulating effects.

However, balance is also important. That means there should be connections between texture, color or form. The space between objects as much as the objects themselves create this harmonious Zen-like state of balance.

ABOVE The round table was the perfect shape for this curved dining room. The triangular grouping of the three pictures manages to reflect this, while retaining the feeling of symmetry. A pair of orchid planters also mirror each other.

LEFT A black runner of stained wood cuts down this circular marble hallway, accentuating the mirroring of furniture and lights on each side. Curved glass panels are set into the atrium above, reflecting the shape of the doors below.

OPPOSITE Symmetry has been created by the construction of the display unit around the television. Only one of the doors at each side leads into another room. The other is there to add balance and conceal the air-conditioning system.

GOLDEN RULES: SYMMETRY AND BALANCE

☆ Use architectural elements or custom-made cabinetry to make a room appear more symmetrical than it is.

☆ Always have a focal point, such as a centrally placed piece of furniture, from which every other element radiates out.

☆ Think of the room as a grid and be aware of the vertical and horizontal lines you are introducing within it.

☆ Once symmetry is in place, introduce an asymmetrical note – conversely, this accentuates the harmony of the room.

☆ Remember that balance is important too – this could be a link between objects of different sizes, or areas where accent color is used.

COLOR AND TEXTURE

1 Contrast is the key word when introducing color and texture. Note the subtle play here between the soft matte of the shaggy goatskin rug and the hard gloss of the wood table. Leather seats with chrome legs reinforce this design idea of textural opposites working together.

2 The same idea is apparent in color. While most of this masculine room is decorated in rich, earthy tones, shots of burnt orange on the velvet pillow and at the windows shake the whole design up, creating more impact.

3 Texture can also be manipulated through lighting. Here a polished leather gentleman's club chair has been given extra depth by light cast from the free-standing lamp. This picks up the orange from the Shoji blinds at the window.

4 The black mirror set into this custom-made radiator cover adds another layer of texture, and also draws the eye back to the goatskin rug – the textural and color anchor of the whole arrangement.

RIGHT When using one dominant color, such as the brown of this urban living room, it is important to introduce as many layers of texture as possible. The goatskin rug is the anchor of the whole interior design, with all the other textural ingredients radiating out from this.

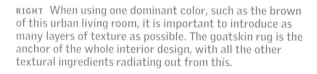

Color and texture

IN DESIGN BOOKS, I HAVE NOTICED THERE IS A PROPENSITY TO SEPARATE COLOR FROM TEXTURE. TO ME, THAT MAKES NO SENSE AT ALL. HOW CAN YOU CHOOSE A COLOR SCHEME WITHOUT A REGARD FOR TEXTURAL ELEMENTS AND THEIR INFLUENCE ON LIGHT AND DARK? HOW CAN YOU CHOOSE A TEXTURE IN ISOLATION FROM THE COLORS THAT SURROUND IT? THE TWO MUST BE CONSIDERED TOGETHER.

It is a common fallacy that colors fall into one of two camps and are either warm or cool. While sand and cream are always warm, shades such as taupe, white and gray – to my mind – can swing in either direction. The secret is to educate your eye to tell a warm-colored white from a cold one, and from there to do the same with other colors. It really isn't difficult: you can learn a lot just by playing around with swatches – find a truly pure white to start with and then place other whites alongside. You will soon start to notice subtle differences – how pink in tone some whites look . . . or yellow, gray, blue and so on.

The other fact to be aware of is that different textures can also introduce notes of warmth or cool into a room. Again, some of these are obvious – cashmere, wool and rich wood are warm; linen, lacquer and marble are cool. Others take more time to understand: velvet, for example, is warm to the touch but can look cool as it shimmers under the light. Murano glass is cool to the touch but can look hot when backlit to show off its wild colors. Part of the fun of putting a design together is playing around with textures. The energy they create gives neutral color schemes a lift and prevents them from lapsing into blandness.

The secret of using colors and textures is not only finding ones that work together visually but having an awareness of the energy they create. So, for example, in a room that is very confident in terms of color – such as white, which is surprisingly extroverted – you might want to introduce softer elements with which it can balance, such as sand tones in warm textures – or you may prefer to accentuate its boldness with a further overlay of white in lacquer, porcelain or satin. It is how you build up the layers of color and texture in a room that determine what overall mood you will create.

Taupe

Taupe is the most perfect neutral color – it is neither too warm nor too cool; it doesn't shriek for attention or feel cloying; it is harmonious, peaceful and Zen.

For me, taupe is the perfect antidote to the stressed and frenetic lives we lead. It instills quietness into a room – a deep sense of calm that restores balance to one's mind. To those coming fresh to the neutral palette, it might also be a surprise to discover how many shades of taupe there are. It is a color that hovers between brown and gray but encompasses many variations in tone. If you find that hard to believe, try experimenting with the swatches. You will soon start to see for yourself that there is a whole mini-spectrum of colors within the taupe family alone.

In fact the only color taupe really doesn't like is yellow, which makes it totally incompatible with sand tones. It is not just that you can't use creamy paint or buttery fabrics in a taupe scheme – you also have to avoid yellowy woods such as oak, yellowy metals such as bronze and yellowy stone such as beige limestone. In my view, taupe and sand are as far removed from each other in design terms as the North and South Poles.

Taupe can be beautifully accessorized with subtle combinations of color and texture; think big urns filled with topiarized moss, silver detailing on mirrors, a collection of paintings all framed in black or the barely-there feel of Plexiglass furniture. Metals such as chrome or stainless steel also feel perfectly at home in a taupe color scheme.

RIGHT In a room that is primarily taupe, textural contrast is key. Here an embroidered bedspread introduces embossed pattern, while sheer curtains and wooden bowls make an interesting play against each other. Color photography is an unexpected addition to the design.

TAUPE LOVES

☆ Pure white paint
☆ Dark-stained wood
☆ Purple undertoned natural linens
☆ Stones that contains gray or blue, such as blue limestone
☆ Metals such as silver and chrome
☆ The companionship of gray or brown
☆ Dramatic accents of green, purple or red
☆ Clear glass

ABOVE LEFT Building up layers of texture is particularly important in an all-taupe room. Here the band of cashmere fabric over the pillow is the same as that on the sofa, while the pillow itself is of contrasting pale taupe linen.

ABOVE RIGHT Pale creams, as opposed to buttery ones, work well with certain shades of taupe – this bedroom is particularly calm and inviting. The cream runner down the bedspread has been sewn in, making it easy to position each morning.

LEFT Taupe comes in many shades. This sumptuous wool bedspread has a dark taupe body and pale taupe border in contrasting satin that drapes on the floor. Dark wood furniture is the anchor in a room built around one color.

BELOW LEFT Taupe is a fabulous detail color too – here the effect of curtains that form pools of texture on the floor are heightened by the band of taupe at the bottom. It makes a graphic statement between the cream fabric and the dark wood floor.

OPPOSITE A dark wood floor makes the ideal anchor to the natural weave used in the chair and the soft two-tone taupe pillow. The chair's texture picks up the fine weave of the carpet and the suede border around it.

TAUPE HATES

☆ Anything that contains yellow, such as buttery paint
☆ Golden woods, such as oak
☆ Yellow-hued linens
☆ Tan leathers
☆ Stones that contains beige
☆ Accessories that hint at yellow, such as dark cream porcelain

ACCESSORIZING TAUPE
One of the perfect companions to taupe is clear glass, because it doesn't compete with its surroundings, but merges with them. It also captures light, which taupe loves. Think tall glass vases, glass lamp bases or even a row of glass jars – simple and inexpensive details that add a further textural twist to the taupe color scheme. Remember too that taupe is fussy about which metals it befriends. Anything with touches of gold or rust is out, but chrome and stainless steel are in. Taupe is also very fond of silver. When it comes to luxury detailing, natural materials such as mother-of-pearl, horn and shagreen are good companions to sophisticated taupe.

TOP LEFT If you want to add interest to a room without using block color, you can opt for a textural finish such as the custom plaster effect in taupe used here. This is very effective in a kitchen built around neutral tones.

TOP CENTER Shoji panels in various shades of neutrals form a backdrop for a simple taupe chair. The feeling created is one of softness and harmony. Mango arum lilies within a tall glass vase harmonize with these colors perfectly.

TOP RIGHT A custom plaster finish has been used on these doors, a way of layering up the taupe color. Note how reflected light increases the feeling of depth. Simple chrome handles are the perfect finishing touch.

ABOVE LEFT Dark wood is the perfect companion to taupe, as shown by the dark-stained mirror propped against this wall that reflects the bed shown opposite. It makes a strong statement against pale taupe walls and carpet.

ABOVE RIGHT Panels of soft taupe-colored wood sets the tone for this bedroom, complemented by pale ivory pillows. Clear glass lamp bases and a Murano glass vase with shades of taupe are perfect accessories in this harmonious interior.

OPPOSITE A heavy velvet dark taupe bedspread is perfect for a winter look. Pale cream on the border and pillows emphasizes its richness both in terms of color and texture. Horn buttons embellish both cream and taupe cushions.

TAUPE ON TAUPE
1. Sisal matting
2. Vintage crushed velvet
3. Natural linen
4. Natural linen
5. Taupe cashmere
6. Dark-stained wood
7. Perfect taupe matte emulsion
8. Shagreen plaster finish
9. Herringbone linen
10. Natural linen
11. Charcoal cashmere

How to design with taupe

ONE OF THE MOST SATISFYING ASPECTS OF WORKING WITH A NEUTRAL COLOR SCHEME IS THAT YOU CAN CHANGE THE LOOK BY INTRODUCING DIFFERENT ACCENT COLORS. TAUPE IS THE PERFECT FOIL FOR THE RICHNESS AND DEPTH OF GREENS, PURPLES AND DARK BROWNS.

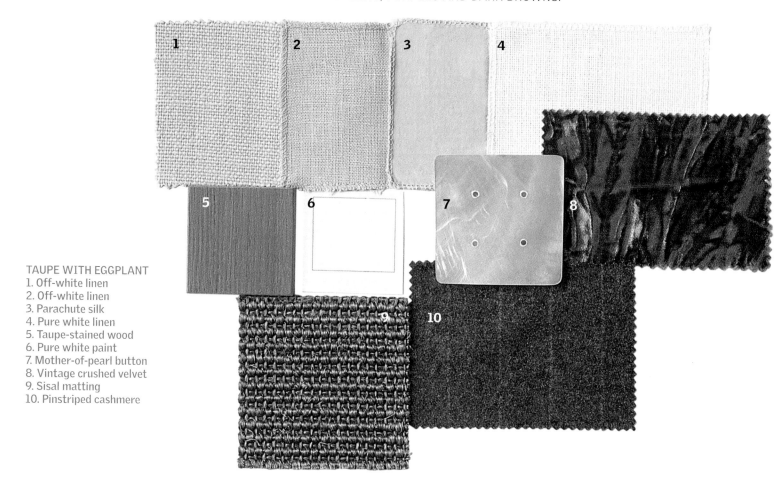

TAUPE WITH EGGPLANT
1. Off-white linen
2. Off-white linen
3. Parachute silk
4. Pure white linen
5. Taupe-stained wood
6. Pure white paint
7. Mother-of-pearl button
8. Vintage crushed velvet
9. Sisal matting
10. Pinstriped cashmere

TAUPE WITH CHOCOLATE
1. Parachute silk
2. Custom plaster finish
3. Natural linen
4. Sisal matting
5. Luster synthetic shot silk
6. Textured taupe linen
7. Horn button
8. Dark-stained wood
9. Faux suede
10. Vintage crushed velvet
11 Boiled wool

TAUPE MIXES

It is possible to create a wonderful interior using nothing but taupe (top left), so long as there is enough textural contrast. Look for opposites – rough with smooth, matte with gloss, opaque and sheer. Here, for example, a robust natural carpet literally grounds the look, providing a foil to shimmery linens and shagreen accessories. An accent color is provided by crushed olive velvet, which picks up the green found in natural linens. Dark-stained wood – with no hint of yellow – is the best choice for a taupe room. If you were to add stone, choose something gray in tone such as gray basalt or slate.

Taupe is the chameleon of colors, taking on a different character depending on its shade, what it is teamed up with and the accent color chosen. It is the perfect foil for grays (left), from pale dove gray to deep charcoal, and the combination results in a mood that is dark, nocturnal and sexy. It is instantly apparent how out of place buttery cream paint would be – whereas pure white is ideal. Purple is a very sensual color, and the perfect accent to introduce here through a fabulous velvet.

Yet another example of taupe's versatility: here a darker taupe palette (above) is offset by bold chocolate tones that sharpen the look, creating a look that is comfortable, warm and versatile. It also dispels the myth that taupe is always cool – this is a very warm color, the perfect antidote to winter weather. In fact the color mix would work as well in a country home as in a more sophisticated urban environment. Red is the perfect accent color – vigorous, energetic and uncompromising. Build on this color theme by introducing accessories such as red art glass vases and vessels in wild, organic shapes, or an installation of fresh red roses.

Sand tones

Sand is warm, comforting and enveloping. It creates an atmosphere that is truly inviting – a place where people feel immediately at ease. It also has practical advantages, being more low-maintenance than other lighter colors, is popular with those with young and energetic families or those in a rural setting. Sand tones have an earthiness that links directly to the natural world.

Men, in particular, are drawn to sand's richness, but there is a danger of it becoming overpowering if you don't hold back a little. For this reason, I often choose sand fabrics that have a hint of pattern, such as a check or stripe, because they break up an expanse of pure sand color in an unobtrusive way.

Just as taupe dislikes sand, so sand never mixes well with taupe. There is a pinkiness in taupe that fights with the yellow in sand. You will never make them friends, so don't waste your time trying. Sand is an easy palette to use with other shades – notably creams, whites and browns. It is also perfect as an accent color; a white room with sand tones will be very different in feel from a room where sand is the dominant shade.

Texture plays a pivotal part in all neutral designs. It is important to use texture boldly where sand is concerned or you could end up with a room that looks flat and characterless. The fact is you can never have too much texture, so juxtapose coarse with delicate, and dense with translucent, in order to give depth to the scheme. If I want to accentuate the richness of sand, I include luxuriously inlaid woods, such as marquetry tables, polished wooden floors or perhaps tan leather furniture or accessories.

RIGHT Sand tones on walls, floor and cabinetry work in perfect harmony in this double-height living room. By choosing cream for the carpet and upholstery – as opposed to caramel – the look stays lighter and more feminine.

TOP RIGHT Sheer Shoji panels provide textural contrast against two dark wood African drums and the matte fabric on the chair. This use of texture is essential in rooms built around one neutral tone, as with the sand shown here.

BELOW RIGHT Accessorizing with art glass is a simple and effective way of introducing other tones into a room – here an organic-shaped vase striped with ochre and chocolate becomes a focal point in a pale sand bathroom.

LEFT This gargantuan headboard not only makes a structural statement within the room, but is a way of introducing bold color. Dark and pale shades of sand fabrics contrast beautifully with the dark wood walls.

TOP LEFT This textured wall has been lightly toned in sand to give extra depth in a small bathroom. The pale cream limestone basin stands out against this, creating a sculptural effect.

BELOW LEFT It is possible to find color contrast within the neutral spectrum. Here rich camel pillows in soft suede add a bolt of color to a pale sand bedroom. Horn buttons on the foldover pillow flaps add textural contrast.

RIGHT Sand is ideal as an accessory color too – here cream pillows have cutouts of sand-colored fabric, which is echoed by upholstery elsewhere in the room. It subtly introduces another layer of color.

ABOVE In the sitting area of a bedroom, panels of rich wood align perfectly with shades of sand. The pale cream lamp shades are made of a sheer silk that bring a sense of lightness into the room.

How to design with sand

THE FIRST CHOICE WHEN DESIGNING WITH SAND IS WHETHER IT WILL BE THE PRIMARY OR SECONDARY COLOR IN THE DESIGN. A ROOM WHERE SAND TONES ARE DOMINANT WILL FEEL VERY DIFFERENT – MORE ENVELOPING – THAN ONE WHERE SAND IS JUST THE ACCENT COLOR SET AGAINST LIGHT AND AIRY CREAM.

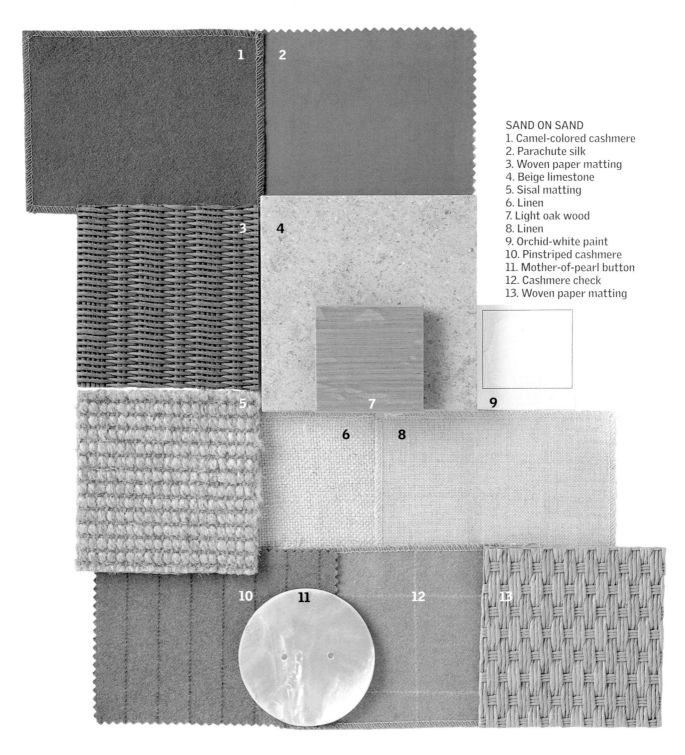

SAND ON SAND
1. Camel-colored cashmere
2. Parachute silk
3. Woven paper matting
4. Beige limestone
5. Sisal matting
6. Linen
7. Light oak wood
8. Linen
9. Orchid-white paint
10. Pinstriped cashmere
11. Mother-of-pearl button
12. Cashmere check
13. Woven paper matting

SAND MIXES

If you like the idea of a room scheme that is predominantly sand, then it is important to include as much textural contrast as possible to prevent the design from looking bland (see left). Here, I have placed rough sisal carpet alongside smooth beige limestone; shiny mother-of-pearl against matte fabrics; and polished wood adjacent to wonderfully tactile woven natural flooring. It is also important to suggest pattern when using sand – just a suggestion of stripes, checks and weaves is enough to add a further layer of interest to the look. When choosing fabrics, make sure you include ones of different weights and compositions in order to introduce even more textural difference. Unlike taupe, sand tones do not sit well alongside the dramatic use of accent colors. Instead it is important to include textural details in complementary tones, such as the mother-of-pearl button shown here. Like sand, materials that link to the natural world

are particularly effective – leather, horn, bronze and ivory are ideal companions for the richness of sand. For the perfect finishing touch, try filling globe glass vases with coral and sand, or displaying simple straight glass vases of orange tiger lilies. Sand is a great color to work with, but if you don't want to use it over a large area, consider making sand the accent color (see below). A cream room with sand tones is one of the easiest to achieve, to live with and to enjoy. Here, the cream carpet makes a clear statement that this is a cream room, while the sand fabrics give depth and definition. When building up a sand-based decorating plan and selecting suitable swatches, you could either opt for cream fabrics and paint colors, such as chalky Chinese porcelain, to add to the light, airy atmosphere, or you could move in the other direction and introduce rust-colored tones to help ground the decorating arrangement with earthy colors.

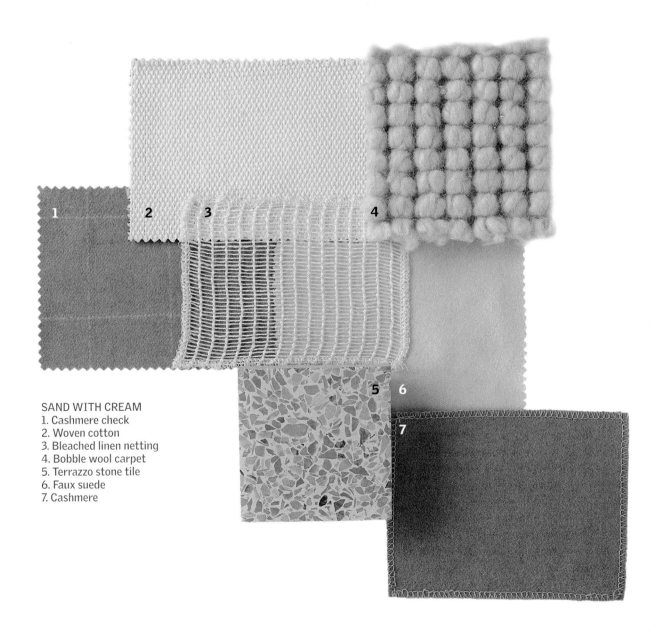

SAND WITH CREAM
1. Cashmere check
2. Woven cotton
3. Bleached linen netting
4. Bobble wool carpet
5. Terrazzo stone tile
6. Faux suede
7. Cashmere

Off-white and cream

Cream is the most tranquil of colors. It is fresh, soft and calming. Walk into a cream room and you can almost feel your pulse slow and your blood pressure lower. There is nothing that will jar the eye or set the spirit on edge.

I have included off-whites here, because they are the bridge between absolutely pure white and cream. They don't have the same richness as cream, but belong to the same family. Off-whites are the perfect companion to creams, not only because they blend with them, but because they prevent a totally cream room from becoming too sickly.

It is because of cream's enveloping nature that you have to be careful what colors to put with it. It works well with navy, black and gray – although a little of these will go a long way. Reds, purples and oranges are not so easy to introduce. Experiment with small touches of these first, rather than taking them too far. Cream is a natural friend to sand tones and browns, but is not so easy to mix with taupe. So, if you want to use natural linens in cream, look for ones that have undertones of green.

Texture is important in any neutral room, but a cream-on-cream one demands more. If everything is blanketed in cream, you must have textural contrast in order to give it a lift. You also have to remember that cream is very affected by natural light – interestingly, it is not the best choice for homes in very sunny climates, because there is a danger of it being fiercely bright, rather than reassuringly calm.

RIGHT Cream is perfect in a room with a lot of natural light but be sure to use different shades of it – as with the banded pillows – or it could look flat and lifeless. Pictures are white-mounted with pale frames to accentuate the overall feeling of airiness.

ABOVE This spectacular dining room has a floor of terrazzo with specks of sand and gray that provides the basis for the design. The dark wooden legs of the chairs add interest by breaking up the cream furniture, walls and fabric.

OPPOSITE TOP LEFT Even something as simple as a pillow can have an effect when seen in the context of a cream-on-cream room. Here fluffy wool contrasts not only with the linen behind it but with shiny horn buttons.

OPPOSITE MIDDLE LEFT Dark wood and sand weave are natural companions to the cream upholstery and slim bolster on this bedroom chair. Textural play continues with the sheer curtains, banded with linen at floor level.

CREAM LOVES

☆ Off-whites, which are its natural companion.
☆ The harmony it creates with sand tones and browns.
☆ Lots of natural light.
☆ Plenty of texture – particularly in cream-on-cream rooms.
☆ Natural linens but ones with green undertones.
☆ Rich-colored woods such as oak.
☆ Touches of navy blue and chocolate brown.

CREAM HATES

☆ Being taken for granted. Using cream does not guarantee success.
☆ Too many buttery shades that have a cloying effect.
☆ Too many silvery metals such as aluminium and stainless steel.
☆ Dark rooms dependent on artificial light.
☆ An overdose of strong reds, purples or oranges.
☆ An overload of dark colors in a predominantly cream scheme.

TOP RIGHT The composition on these floating shelves is a way of breaking up a look that is predominantly cream – chrome, clear glass, ceramics, books and a painting propped up create a textural play against each other.

BOTTOM RIGHT In a room that combines different gradients of cream, the canvas above the fireplace and the headboard are relatively dark – anchoring to the room. Venetian mirrors have an invisible quality that works well here.

Pure whites

This is a fabulous color to design with - clean, fresh, summery, spiritual and totally life-enhancing. It always surprises me when people don't view white as a "proper" color. To me, it is one of the most vibrant and energetic shades. It is far more dramatic than cream, which is why the off-whites belong there and not with the pure whites.

White is unashamedly glamorous and high maintenance, and so has come to denote luxury. However, the fact is that more people now "zone" their homes, often treating themselves to a master bedroom or private sitting room devoted to white. White-on-white is one of my favorite combinations (there are literally hundreds of shades to choose from), but as with cream rooms, it is important to have a lot of textural contrast. You can even introduce a layer of texture through the way natural light enters the room – shadows from shuttered blinds, for example, look wonderful against a white carpet. In my mind I equate white with soft, floaty, almost transparent fabrics – imagine clouds of parachute silk. But it also translates well into soft velvets or matte leathers.

White is a truly versatile color. Taupe and sand may work against each other, but white works happily with both. It also loves bold accent colors, such as red, purple or navy blue. In fact the only color I would hold back on is black, which can look too harsh with pure white. Black-framed artwork is the exception, because it creates good graphic shapes against the wall. When it comes to accessories, almost anything goes, but white lacquer, clear glass or accent colors of vibrant fresh flowers are particularly effective.

RIGHT Accent color is the perfect way of changing the look of a room that is predominantly white. Pillows and flowers can be switched according to season, while the art installation provides the only permanent strong color.

THE ART BOOK

Pica

PURE WHITE LOVES

☆ Taupe – to which it adds contrast.
☆ Sand – to which it adds freshness.
☆ Neutrals such as gray to which it gives a lift.
☆ Bold accent colors of red or orange.
☆ Pale stones, such as Thassos marble or white ceramic tiles.
☆ Bleached or painted wood.
☆ Floaty fabrics.
☆ See-through accessories, such as clear glass or Plexiglas.

TOP LEFT Pure white works happily with off-white neutrals, such as the limestone basin and bath shown here against white tiled walls. A slim floating shelf in natural wood and chrome accessories, break up the expanse of white.

TOP RIGHT Black backdrops in these bold paintings have visual impact in a white-on-white room. Too much black and too much color can look harsh in such a design, so be cautious when introducing it – one accent color can be enough.

LEFT Venetian blinds in pure white have an architectural quality that is accentuated here by the graphic quality of the lamp. The way light falls into the room, filtered through slats, softens the pure white shades used in the interior.

PURE WHITE HATES

☆ Too much yellowy cream.
☆ Too many different colors mixed together.
☆ Too much black.
☆ Insufficient natural light.
☆ Children and pets.
☆ The pollution of the city – it is a better choice for a vacation home.

LEFT In a pure white room, very little color is needed to have a striking effect. Here a Chinese red headboard in matte velvet lifts the look, picked up only by two of the pillows and the line of red Singapore orchids in vases at the foot of the bed.

ABOVE The way light falls has an enormous effect on all colors, white included. Here sunlight is bright and glittering on this Thassos marble floor, but in the evening the effect becomes cooler and softer changing the mood entirely.

The glass frame of this free-standing mirror has an invisible quality that complements the loose, unlined curtains perfectly. Off-white walls make the ideal canvas for natural tones of oatmeal, sand and gray, while the dark wood headboard provides an anchor.

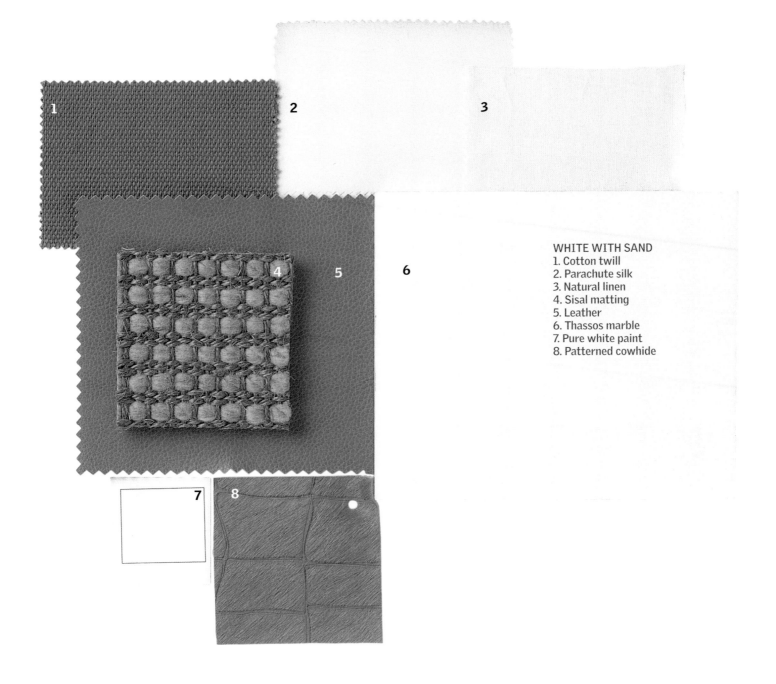

WHITE WITH SAND
1. Cotton twill
2. Parachute silk
3. Natural linen
4. Sisal matting
5. Leather
6. Thassos marble
7. Pure white paint
8. Patterned cowhide

How to design with white

WHITE IS A DREAM TO WORK WITH AS LONG YOU OFFER ENOUGH TEXTURAL CONTRAST. NAVY BLUE, CHARCOAL GREY, BRIGHT RED AND BURNT ORANGE ARE ALL EXCELLENT ACCENT COLORS TO OFFSET PURE WHITE.

WHITE MIXES well with both the taupe and sand families. In a pure white room, sand will work as a great accent color, because it helps to ground the look adding depth and contours. It also alters the mood: a white-on-white room is both decadent and glamorous; sand introduces a more relaxed, laid-back natural feel. It's the difference between wearing a pure white trouser suit and a crisp white shirt worn with moleskin trousers. Here, the core of the room is pure white (see above): white marble, white walls and white sheer curtains at the window, but sand linens and leather upholstery help to soften the overall effect and make it appear less clinical. Horn, bronze and white lacquer detailing are textural additions worth considering and would all work perfectly in this interior design.

LIGHTING PLANS

Lighting design

GOOD LIGHTING IS ABOUT REFLECTING YOUR MOOD,
AND ACKNOWLEDGING THAT THIS MOOD MAY
GRADUALLY SHIFT AND CHANGE THROUGHOUT THE DAY.

Lighting is the sexier side of interior design and, over the last decade, there has been an incredible shift in the way that lighting is perceived. Good lighting design is now something that people are prepared to spend money on, even if it means having to make savings elsewhere.

You can buy lighting systems that preset moods for morning, midday, early evening and nighttime. It might sound rather robotic,

but in fact there is something incredibly soothing about being able to change the atmosphere in a room just by pressing some numbers into a keypad. The simple truth is that if you have great lighting in your home, you don't need much else at all – most of what we put into our homes is icing, but lighting is part of the cake.

Having said that, there is no reason to over-complicate your lighting plan. The mistake that many people make is to overdo it and spend money unnecessarily. A good lighting consultant will ask you questions about the way you and your family live. Beware of those who simply talk about the amazing effects that they can create; after all, you do not want your home turned into a nightclub! The lighting should enhance the way you live in a comfortable, relaxed way.

GOLDEN RULES: LIGHTING

1 Lighting is a clever way of throwing the viewer's attention on to different parts of a room. The fiber-optic lighting built into the shelves is perfect for mood lighting because when evening comes, it is possible to turn down other lighting in the room and enjoy the effect of walls washed in soft light.

2 A row of metal sculptural lights above the fireplace throws interesting shadows onto the wall, adding depth to the room. This type of lighting is comparable with an art installation because it provides visual impact rather than practicality.

3 Reading is an activity common to living rooms, but it is important to have a light correctly positioned in order not to strain the eyes. This sculptural free-standing light looks wonderful, but is positioned so it can be put to good use, as and when it is needed.

4 The sculptural light on the side table gives off very little illumination, but like those above the fireplace, that is not the primary intention – when other lights are turned off at night, it helps to create a calm, relaxing atmosphere.

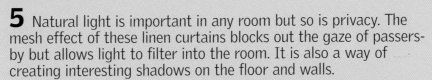

5 Natural light is important in any room but so is privacy. The mesh effect of these linen curtains blocks out the gaze of passers-by but allows light to filter into the room. It is also a way of creating interesting shadows on the floor and walls.

LEFT In a room with good lighting , it is not necessary to spend much money on decorative ingredients. Here plain walls take on a new beauty when washed with light, providing an attractive backdrop for simple glass and a collection of trophies.

LIGHTING DESIGN

The easiest way to understand what is needed is to take a blueprint and – with the help of your architect – use pencil lines to show where light falls naturally and then, in a different color, where more light is needed. It is all about balance. If you light one side of the room well and the other poorly, the end result will not look right.

Don't assume that something as simple as a spotlight will always be purely functional. Directed at a piece of art, it can give incredible depth. For example, I have seen black-and-white photographs of flowers lit up so well you could almost imagine they were opening up in front of your eyes. Using light to highlight certain art or objects not only turns them into a feature, but is a way of disguising architectural faults within a room by turning the attention elsewhere.

TOP You can never have too much light – this huge glass skylight allows natural light to flood into the dining room, boosting light entering through the windows. The skylight is actually the glass floor of a veranda overhead.

ABOVE A view down a first floor landing to the atrium above a hallway: glass panels at waist height allow a clear view through to the incredible chandelier – like an upside-down wedding cake – and the windows beyond.

LEFT It is possible to "borrow" light from other rooms by making architectural changes, such as cutting out a panel in a wall – this window allows light from an adjacent staircase and hall into a somewhat dark basement kitchen.

OPPOSITE This passageway has very little natural light, so artificial lighting has been well used on the ceiling and walls; by lighting the photographs from behind, it appears they are glowing when other lights are switched off.

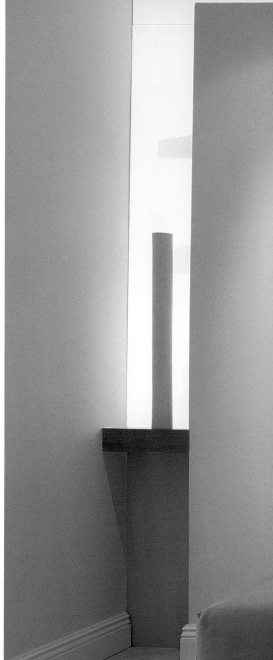

Lighting falls into three main categories: task, mood and decorative. The following rules apply to every space in the house: first determine what activities take place there; then decide what lighting is needed for those activities; assess what is already in place and what is needed to enhance it. You might feel you have enough technical knowledge to take on the lighting yourself – and certainly there are now great designs available everywhere – but if you can afford it, I would always recommend using a lighting designer. The reason for this is that he or she will not only help you understand what is needed but will think of wonderfully inventive ways to achieve it. Lighting when done well is a form of sculpture. It is not just about beams of light but about silhouettes and shadows, flooding the walls in one place and creating cutout effects in another, juxtaposing cold light with warm light, borrowing natural light by adding a glass skylight or partially knocking out a wall, diffusing light through sand-blasted glass or thin gauze, bouncing light off mirrors or catching it in prisms of crystal. This is what makes it so sexy: its ability not only to transform a space, but to be transformed according to different materials. Forget paintings. Forget lush fabrics. Forget one-of-a-kind designer pieces. If you want to make a startling difference to your home, lighting is where it is at.

TOP LEFT By fitting the cabinetry in this bedroom slightly away from the wall, as opposed to flush against it, it is possible to fit custom lighting behind which makes the cabinetry appear to glow. The table lamp then plays on this idea by casting light onto the wood.

BELOW LEFT Architectural elements in this double-height room are accentuated by the use of well-positioned lighting. This makes a feature of the cabinetry and draws the eye upwards, emphasizing the scale of the space.

ABOVE This wall appears to float in front of an illuminated partition wall, adding depth to the room. The photographs are lit from below, washing the surface in light and creating an interesting effect of shadow and light.

RIGHT In contemporary artwork, such as this canvas of slits and rips, the shadows produced are part of the total effect. Special lighting has been positioned on the floor to accentuate the three-dimensional nature of the piece.

DECORATIVE LIGHTING

DECORATIVE LIGHTING

The other main development in lighting over the last few years has been the way it has been embraced by furniture and product designers as an exciting form of interior sculpture. Light fixtures can become the unique focal point of a room, enhancing a space with glamour or decadence.

For focal points to have optimum impact, you must already have the core arrangement of task and mood lighting in place. Something striking to the eye is not necessarily relevant in terms of function; you must think of it as an additional piece of art in the room. Ceiling lights, for example, fell out of favor because the light they cast was flat and diffused. Now they have become highly chic, but that is because they are additional to the main lighting scheme, and the light they cast is aesthetic rather than practical.

Decorative lighting falls into two distinct categories: pieces that create wonderful lighting effects; and those that are themselves intrinsically beautiful objects. Of all the ceiling lights to shout wow,

TOP LEFT Chandeliers are an enduring favorite with those that love lighting because the way that light plays on crystals is so pretty. Contemporary versions such as this have lost none of the romance that such designs evoke.

TOP CENTER Wall lights are an effective addition to a lighting plan, but must be hung at a height in proportion to the rest of the room. This bronze design with parchment shade is elegant and unobtrusive.

TOP RIGHT Fine porcelain tiles overlaid on each other have been used to construct this unusual wall light through which there is a glow of illumination. It is both a beautiful effect and an eye-catching design.

BOTTOM LEFT This sculptural wall light in bronze and parchment has an organic feel that contrasts well with symmetrically hung photographs. The juxtaposition of light against picture creates an interesting composition on the wall.

BOTTOM CENTER This free-standing floor light is a contemporary version of the traditional standard lamp. The crystal shade creates a glittering effect, while allowing the eye to look through to the window treatments beyond.

BOTTOM RIGHT This unusual fabric light echoes the narrow proportions of a corridor with doors on both sides. It is a good example of how a light can be both functional and sculptural, creating a focus in an otherwise uninteresting space.

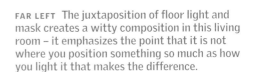

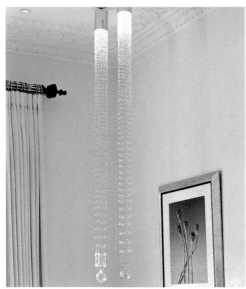

FAR LEFT The juxtaposition of floor light and mask creates a witty composition in this living room – it emphasizes the point that it is not where you position something so much as how you light it that makes the difference.

CENTER LEFT Colored lamps that appear to glow are perfect in a child's bedroom, adding fun and a sense of security at night. Their toadstool shape and bold colors link to the gnomes sitting nearby.

ABOVE This flat metal wall light is so modernist that it replaces conventional artwork. For best effect, other lights in the room are dimmed so that its aesthetic impact can be fully appreciated.

LEFT Stunning sculptural lights constructed from slender cylinders of glass have been hung asymmetrically in an otherwise symmetrical room. This actually draws the eye towards them, making them more of a focal point in the plan.

OPPOSITE A metal lamp shade casts shadows onto the walls of this elegant living room when lit, creating a really theatrical effect. When not in use, it is as though its figurative design dances ghost-like on the walls.

the chandelier is king. Glass and crystal are highly seductive materials and contemporary designers love the effect they have on light. Glittering antique ones look fabulous in starkly modern interiors, but chandeliers have also been reinvented in wonderful new ways to become edgy, urban focal pieces. It is not just what they are made of that makes them interesting, but the tiered form. They are particularly effective in halls, where they mirror the shape of stairs spiraling down. Wrapping them in gauze or very fine linen accentuates their seductive shape.

Wall lights too have taken on new relevance, having discarded their rather suburban image. However, of all lighting this is the one easiest to get wrong. Placing them at the right height is key – they must fit with the proportions of the room both vertically and horizontally. They also need to be balanced throughout a space, otherwise the whole scheme will appear out of kilter.

The use of fiber optics are set to revolutionize decorative lighting even further over the next few years. Light is transmitted down glass fibers, but no heat or UV rays are emitted, making it perfect for using with fabrics or other delicate materials. It is also useful for providing light in places where access is problematic. I sometimes use fiber optics to light the back of glass backsplashes in kitchens, for example, or sandwich them between glass and linen on closet doors. Decorative lighting is a joy to use – like adding jewels to a really classic outfit. You don't need much to make an impact, but you want people to notice the ones you have.

Room details

 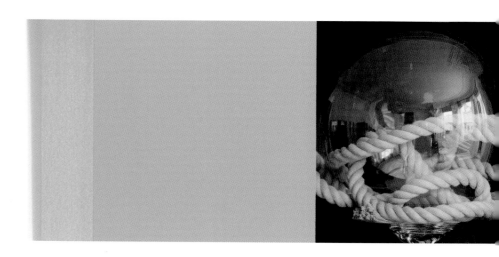

CABINETRY UPHOLSTERY CURTAINS

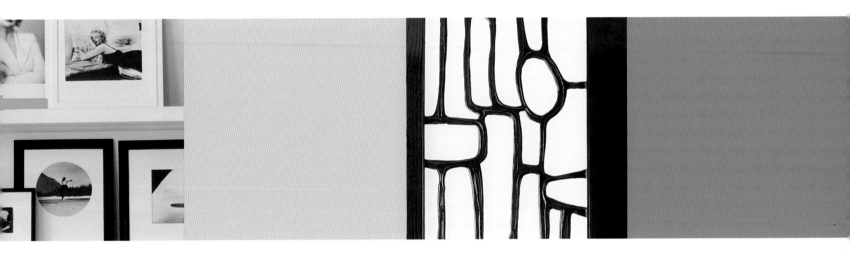

BLINDS PILLOWS THROWS RUNNERS

THIS IS THE PART OF THE BOOK YOU HAVE PROBABLY BEEN LONGING TO REACH – THE FUN PART. ASSUMING SPATIAL PROBLEMS HAVE BEEN OVERCOME, THE USE OF THE ROOM HAS BEEN AGREED, QUESTIONS OF MOOD AND BALANCE DISCUSSED, AND SUITABLE LIGHTING INSTALLED – IT IS NOW TIME TO COMMISSION CABINETRY, UPHOLSTERY, HOME FURNISHINGS AND ALL THE OTHER DECORATIVE TOUCHES THAT MAKE A HOME TRULY YOUR OWN. BE WARNED THOUGH; WITH SO MANY STYLES TO CHOOSE FROM, THIS CAN BE A BEWILDERING TIME. YOU ARE NOW AT YOUR MOST VULNERABLE. EVERY DECISION YOU MAKE WILL LEAVE YOU WONDERING WHETHER IT IS THE RIGHT ONE. A VISIT TO A FRIEND'S HOUSE OR A NEW SHOP CAN LEAVE YOU ANXIOUS AND FEELING THAT YOU ARE COMPLETELY ON THE WRONG PATH. THAT IS WHY IT IS SO IMPORTANT TO PUT TOGETHER

FABRIC, FLOORING AND PAINT SWATCHES FOR EACH ROOM YOU ARE DECORATING ON A BOARD, AS SHOWN IN THE CHAPTER ON COLOR AND TEXTURE (SEE PAGES 72-99), BECAUSE THEY ACT AS TANGIBLE REMINDERS OF YOUR OVERALL VISION. THE IMPORTANT THING TO REMEMBER IS THAT SOME OF THESE DECORATIVE CHOICES ARE MORE BINDING THAN OTHERS. CABINETRY, FOR EXAMPLE, IS BOTH EXPENSIVE AND IMPRACTICAL TO CHANGE, WHEREAS A NEW SET OF PILLOWS WILL HARDLY RUIN THE BUDGET. IF YOU ARE WORKING AROUND EXISTING FURNITURE, IT IS IMPORTANT TO PLACE A SAMPLE OF THIS ON THE DESIGN BOARD FIRST. WHEN PLANNING THE LOOK OF A ROOM, I LIKE TO START BY CHOOSING MY FABRICS, BECAUSE PAINT AND CARPET COLORS ARE RELATIVELY EASY TO ADD TO THESE. AS YOU WORK, TRY TO VISUALIZE THE FINISHED ROOM IN YOUR HEAD.

CABINETRY AND DOORS

CABINETRY is one of the most expensive ingredients in the home. Not only is the wood and other specialized materials expensive, but the custom-made element of good cabinetry means labor costs are very high. It is possible to buy ready-made storage systems that look great, but nothing compares to the couture element of built-ins produced to fit your own personal specifications.

The real joy of having cabinetry made to order is that it will provide a space for everything you wish to store, and allow you to live a freer, less cluttered existence.

You can change your mind a million times about fabric, furniture or paint shade, but once you have decided on wood for cabinetry you have set a tone for the room. This is often a concern for people who move into a house where the cabinetry is well made, but not a shade of wood they like. They think they will be able to work around it by adding other colors or textures. Take it from me: this will

never work. You must either stain the wood dark – something people resist doing to "good" hardwoods such as oak or mahogany, rip it all out and start again regardless of "waste," or design an arrangement that is sympathetic to that particular wood.

Remember too that built-ins are not just about storage, but about display and concealment too. They can incorporate obvious elements such as bookcases or floating shelves and less obvious ones such as fish tanks and sculpture pedestals. It can also be used to camouflage unsightly air-conditioning units or the ubiquitous home entertainment system.

OPPOSITE Cabinetry covers one wall of this living room, providing custom-made housing for television and audio equipment. The gray panels are actually loud speakers covered in linen gauze, which integrate so well they add a decorative element.

BELOW LEFT In this dressing room, the cabinets are custom-made to include different drawer sizes for various items of clothing. It is not necessary to choose handles that all look the same – here a long, thin handle is used alongside small, rounded door knobs.

LEFT Invisible doors can trick the eye into thinking something is more solid than it is. Cabinetry has been used here to conceal unsightly air-conditioning equipment but appears to be a style statement within the room.

BELOW RIGHT By commissioning built-ins it is possible to make use of every corner of the room – here a cabinet of shallow drawers has been made to fit into a narrow alcove. Note how the cupboard to the left neatly follows the line of the slanting roof eaves.

DOORS are the most dominant feature of built-ins. In rooms such as the bedroom or dressing room, they can take up a huge expanse of wall space that is hard to visualize at the planning stage. I like big solid blocks of texture or color, but not everyone does. One of the reasons for introducing a textural mix into doors, such as wood with cane, dark wood with leather, or glass with gauze, is that it breaks up what can appear to be a somewhat monolithic structure.

However, try not to worry when you see cabinetry in place for the first time. In effect, it is like building a huge box within a room, so understandably you will feel that the walls have closed in on you. Give it a couple of days and the eye will adjust and you will feel that the boundaries have melted away again and become less dominant.

Built-ins are not designed in isolation from the rest of the room; they are absolutely central to a design concept. That means doors must relate to other items within the room, through color, texture or shape. It also means that knobs cannot be added as an afterthought. They are as central to the design as the wood you choose, and must be part of the design from the beginning. If you want doors that blend into the walls as though invisible, choose ones that need no knobs – such as sliding or pivoting doors. But if you want them to become a decorative feature within the room, choose luxurious knobs that embellish the look.

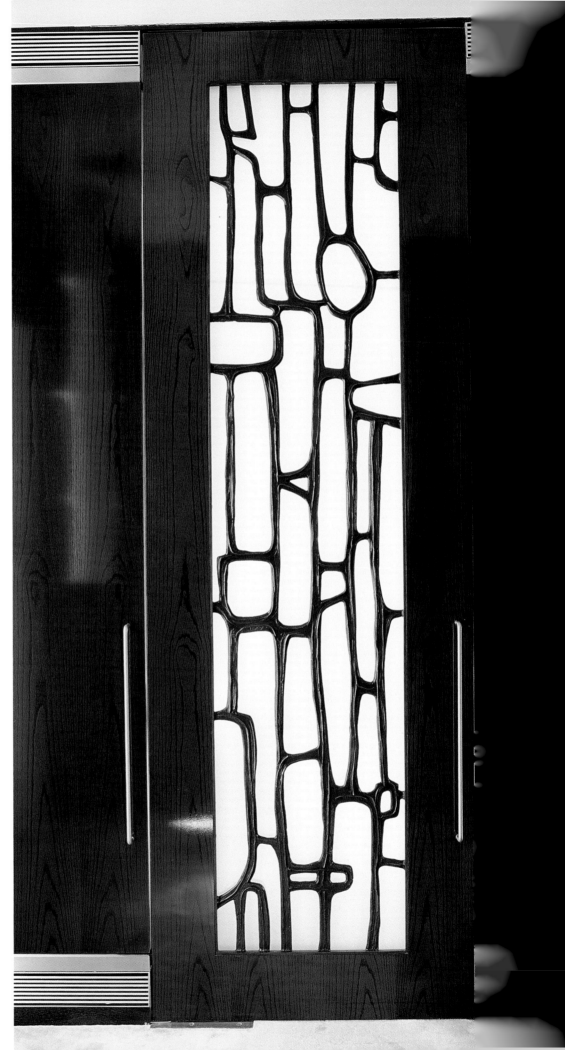

ABOVE Starkly black floor-to-ceiling cupboards with sliding doors create an architectural effect in the entrance to a bathroom. The grooves add extra interest to the surface, which has a slight sheen to it, allowing light to reflect.

RIGHT This door reaches up to the ceiling and would have made the room feel claustrophobic had it been solid. Instead custom ironwork has been commissioned to form ornate panels in the glass, transforming it into a decorative element.

OPPOSITE TOP LEFT Pivot doors are an effective way of dividing rooms when needed or allowing the view to continue through to the adjoining space. The tall slender door handles echo the elongated paneled windows in surrounding walls.

OPPOSITE TOP CENTER It is important to consider not only the style of doors but their method of opening. Here sliding doors along one wall double as screens in this sleek interior, allowing adjoining rooms to be either separated or integrated.

OPPOSITE TOP RIGHT Specially made oval handles that embellish otherwise flat floor-to-ceiling cupboards become the main decorative ingredient in this Eastern inspired hall. Opaque panels of glass set into the door accentuate this Eastern style.

OPPOSITE BOTTOM LEFT Small, subtle lights set near the floor are a way of marking the perimeters between doors in this elegant hall. They also cast a soft light onto the floor, which is picked up by the large oval doorstop of polished lignum vitae.

OPPOSITE BOTTOM RIGHT Custom-made handles can be used to imprint the surrounding woodwork with character and interest – here simple rectangular shapes made of matching metal stress the geometry of full height doors set flush to the wall.

LEFT A wall of matte silk conceals a door, made visible only by the crystal doorknob. The upholstered finish not only adds textural interest, but also creates pattern along the passage. An extra deep entrance also adds interest.

OPPOSITE RIGHT Cream leather inlays lighten and soften the cabinetry in this dressing room, and echo the cream leather topped dresser. Handles have not been used on the cupboards since they would break up the streamlined design.

OPPOSITE BELOW LEFT A small room of solid doors can feel very overpowering, so paneling is ideal in a space such as a dressing room. Here leather handles and rattan paneling complement the wood, introducing texture as well as creating an interesting visual effect.

OPPOSITE BELOW RIGHT A full-length mirror has become a focal point within a bedroom by surrounding it with rich wood from floor to ceiling. A row of small pictures at each side play with the idea of scale.

CUSTOM CABINETRY sits at the couture end of interior design. Just as high-end fashion is quickly picked up and turned around by department stores, so decorative interior that were once the domain of the very rich are now more easily accessible. One such example is the vogue for custom upholstery, such as leather, on doors. You no longer need to have these custom-made; there are plenty of shops that will make them to order. This kind of style statement has to be absolutely perfect – material that has bubbled or pulled will spoil the effect so, if you do find a talented upholsterer, hang on to them.

You also have to be very sure it is what you want. It will be an expensive addition to your home, so it is not the sort of thing you want to tire of in a few months time. There is also a maintenance factor to consider – I always recommend faux leather, for example, because it is easier to clean and similarly, you must ensure that leather doors, which are in constant use, are not going to show fingerprints after a year or so.

Having said all of that, there is no doubt that the end result is very attractive. Cabinetry is a very hard element within a room and this is a way of softening the sheer volume of so much wood. Texture is also an integral part of any design and special finishes, such as these, are a way of introducing an additional layer of interest.

Custom cabinetry also allows you to introduce subtle visual references. It might be, for example, that the overall look is oriental, in which case doors can add an Eastern touch – perhaps through nothing more than the shape of a door handle. It could be that the style is absolutely minimalist, in which case they can be made to fit tight to the corners with no handles or embellishments to break the lines.

Whereas cabinetry has as much to do with the interior of a piece of furniture as the exterior, doors are one of the most important pieces of internal architecture – whether connecting rooms or concealing cupboards. Because they are such a dominant feature, their appearance throughout the home should be considered. Custom work allows you to achieve this level of consistency and flawlessness.

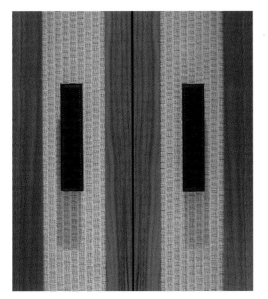

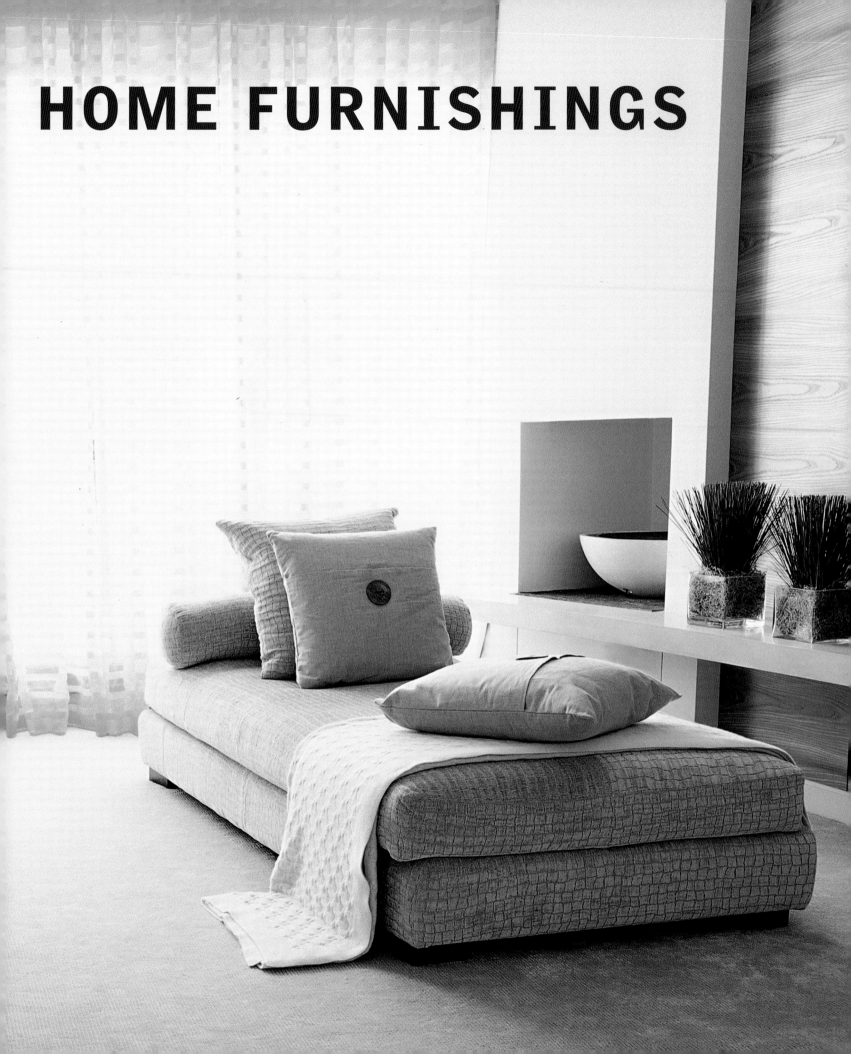

HOME FURNISHINGS

Green Shoji panels are the focus in this living room, setting the tone for colors in the upholstery and table through to the pillows and art glass. The use of white linen on the pillows and chair is the perfect foil to the sharpness of bright apple green.

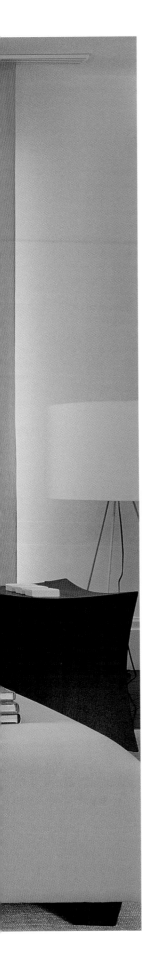

Using fabric

PEOPLE OFTEN THINK THAT DESIGN IS ONLY ABOUT THE LOOK OF A ROOM, BUT IN FACT IT IS MORE ABOUT HOW A ROOM FEELS. IT IS FABRIC THAT CONVEYS MOOD, WHICH IS WHY WHEN DESIGNING A ROOM, MY STARTING POINT IS ALWAYS FABRIC.

It is not enough to arrange fabric swatches on a design board that work together in terms of tone; there should also be a chemistry between them that will put a certain signature on the room. Fabrics used in interior designs are no different than those used in fashion: denim denotes casual, just as taffeta shouts luxury or sheepskin suggests rustic. You can play with this idea of the character of the fabric by bringing together those that alter each other's "personality." I might, for example, take a very grand fabric, such as a Fortuny silk, and place it next to a modest muslin. The silk loses none of its beauty and the muslin none of its simplicity, but the effect they create in combination is quite different than using only one of them in isolation.

Fabrics are also the perfect way of reflecting the seasons. In the summer, what can be better than waking up to white sheer curtains at the window that float in the breeze? In the winter, it is wonderful to sit by a fire wrapped in a wool blanket or throw. The hard elements of a room, such as floor and cabinetry, are fixed – but it is relatively inexpensive to change your home furnishings for different times of the year.

Remember too that fabrics are organic in structure. A grid system is the perfect foundation for design and soft furnishings can reinforce these horizontal and vertical lines in an interior through the use of hanging banners and table runners, but ultimately fabrics are there to blur those hard edges. When you walk into a room, the choice and use of fabrics should make you feel enveloped in softness and harmony.

GOLDEN RULES: HOME FURNISHINGS

1 Banded pillows are an ideal way of unifying different colors and textures within a room. The green band over this white linen pillow makes a link to the pillow behind, but is also a direct reflection of the green and white of the Shoji panels.

2 By using Shoji panels in linen and cotton, in two contrasting shades – white and green – the room has been given a very defined linear structure. The horizontal line of the upholstered table cuts across this forming the core grid of the room's design.

3 When using one dominant color on all the key pieces of furniture, it is important to alter textures. The matte raw silk of the ottoman works beautifully with the chenille on the sofa and silk and linen pillows. Both black and white have been used to accessorize.

4 A high-backed chair with a slip cover of white linen introduces a note of softness that breaks up the grids of the room. Pure white is a surprisingly dominant color, which draws the eye to it, so it can be used sparingly.

WINDOW TREATMENTS

WINDOW TREATMENTS are not only an important focal point within a room, they also have a practical use – shutting out light and keeping in warmth. Your first consideration, therefore, is whether you like to sleep in total darkness and want something that blacks out morning light, or whether you enjoy sunlight flooding through the windows at the start of the day. If you have double glazing, warmth should not be an issue – but if not, you may have to allow for lined or thicker curtains.

Japanese-style blinds are a favorite window solution of mine because they offer enormous versatility. The Velcro attachments mean you can easily change them according to mood or season, so you might opt for sheer one day and leather the next. They also create strong graphic lines, which makes them ideal for use in a room where you want to achieve an ordered, linear look.

Curtains have a more organic quality than blinds, particularly if left long and allowed to fall to the floor in pools of fabric, or are lightweight enough to gently flutter in the breeze. Remember though that when curtains are drawn, they create a block effect of color and pattern. That means you have to choose a design that looks good when seen as a large expanse. Neutrals are best since you are less likely to tire of them quickly.

Blinds or shutters are a practical solution in rooms where curtains are not an option, either because of fit or function. For example

LEFT The same sheer fabric in two different shades has been chosen for Shoji panels here, so that where they overlap less light comes in. This combination introduces color, texture and pattern, as well as creating interesting effects of natural light.

RIGHT Shoji panels of burnt orange mohair and sheer black emphasize the masculine tone of this Japanese-inspired room. Charcoal-colored wooden orchid holders provide textural contrast both to lacquered furniture and translucent fabric.

GOLDEN RULES: WINDOWS

☆ In a room where you want to stress architectural elements, choose blinds or panels that reinforce the lines in the space.

☆ Consider not only how curtains or blinds will look by day, but the effect of blocks of color or pattern when drawn at night.

☆ In a double-glazed room – where curtains do not need to insulate the room – consider just the visual – sheer silk falling to the floor perhaps?

☆ If you do not want to block out too much natural light but retain privacy, choose fabrics that mix matte with sheer, such as cotton and voile.

☆ Finials and rods are an important part of the window treatment and should also link to other design elements within the room.

ABOVE Shoji panels are extremely versatile and can be used as room dividers as well as for window dressing. These ones separate a dressing room from a bedroom – when one room is lit and the other is dark, they help create mood.

TOP RIGHT Simple top treatments can be very pleasing. Here a thin stainless-steel rod threaded through eyelets at the top of curtains gives a pleated look to the fabric. A border in a darker tone accentuates this effect.

BELOW RIGHT An accordion effect is created by this smart two-tone curtain gracing a small bathroom window. A blind would have been the conventional choice, but this creates a more interesting, three-dimensional result.

in attic rooms on sloping dormer windows. If you choose a shutter in a hard material, such as wood, balance it with something much more tactile elsewhere in the room, such as a rich velvet upholstery fabric on a chair.

Window treatments can never be designed in isolation from the rest of the home furnishings in a room. There must be links between the different elements, although these should never be as obvious as the over-coordinated home furnishing trend popular twenty years ago. It is simply a question of striking a visual balance. It may be that the curtain fabric in a bedroom is echoed by a runner going down a headboard, for example, or a panel of fabric across a pillow. Or it might be that a fabric blind is subtly mirrored in a throw over a chair back or the fabric of a table runner.

Finally, do not overlook decorative details like finials and curtain rods. Their appearance should link to elements elsewhere in the room, particularly woodwork. Cabinets with sharp, straight lines should be complemented by similarly unfussy curtain rods. The finials are like placing jewels with an outfit – a place where you can add a touch of fun or glamor. If, for example, you have designed a bathroom with lots of glass, choose a rod with sparkling glass finials. The important thing is to find subtle visual links between one part of a room and another.

Curtains can be for display rather than for function. This airy parachute silk falls in pools of fabric to the floor, like a bridal dress, creating both textural and color contrast against the crisp black lacquered wood of the steps.

ABOVE The sheen on this luxurious white shot silk bedspread picks up natural light, creating pools of brightness and shadow on its surface. Sand-colored pillows break up its expanse, providing an anchor to the color scheme.

RIGHT An upholstered panel of sand linen built into a wall could be a piece of artwork, but in fact doubles up as a functional headboard. Pillows are kept to the minimum in order not to detract from its simple shape.

HEADBOARDS AND COVERS

I absolutely love oversized headboards – the taller, the better. They are the focal point of the bedroom; the first thing you see when you walk into the room. Although you can buy very chic ready-made designs, it is also possible to have ones custom-made at little extra cost. After all, inexpensive particleboard is perfectly suitable as the base and can be cut to size, over which you can use the most luxurious fabrics – anything from slip covers of antique linen or cashmere to fitted fake ostrich skin or suede.

Not that headboards are the only solution. You might want to fix an inlaid panel of wood or lacquer over the bed – creating a sort of art installation. Or you could be very minimalist and simply suggest a headboard with a row of pillows. It really comes down to the mood you want to create in this particular room.

When considering bedding, runners work well, but the trick is to have them sewn into the bedspread. Life is simply too short to make the bed each morning and spend ages trying to position a runner in the right place. The beauty of introducing another fabric into an existing plain bedspread is that it offers an opportunity to play with textures by juxtaposing light with dark or smooth with rough. Remember though that each fabric used should link in some way to another part of the room.

Bedcovers are an easy home furnishing to change according to the season. In summer, nothing feels better than crisp white sheets and goosedown. In winter, it is lovely to snuggle under layers of wool or velvet (but make sure they won't feel itchy). Remember though it is easy to get carried away by the look of a room, but you should never sacrifice comfort for aesthetics. Just as a headboard should be firm enough to give support and soft enough to be relaxing, so a bedspread should be warm, but not too heavy. Even in winter, you don't want to feel as if you are sleeping under a deadweight of covers. Bedrooms should be about luxury and feeling pampered – and nothing will influence that more than the fabrics you choose.

ABOVE A cream headboard in faux baby ostrich is the epitome of indulgence, and also luxury. Vintage velvet cushions in moss green add a further note of decadence to soft cream bedding and pillows.

TOP LEFT The bedroom is the perfect place to reflect changing moods between seasons. This sheepskin throw is perfect for cozy nights in winter, as are layers of pillows in comforting and enveloping colors.

BELOW LEFT A paneled headboard reflects the grid structure that underlies the room's design. This is echoed by the way pillows are arranged from large bolster to banded square, to small bolster and small square.

PILLOWS AND BOLSTERS

A pillow is so much more than people imagine. It is a way of introducing a shot of color or pattern into a room; it can be used to create an additional layer of texture; depending on its size, it can help you play tricks with scale; and it can be made in any shape you desire. It is also cheap enough to enable you to change the look of a room entirely by replacing one set of pillows with another – and reflecting that change through accessories. Yet people rarely give the humble cushion the same attention as the rest of their home furnishings.

Cushions also offer a peep-hole into your personality. Are you the sort of person who likes them conventionally square in shape and in one fabric? Do you like to use them big, in colors that shriek? Or do you love them banded, buttoned 'n braided and dressed up? There is no right or wrong here; it is all about what you are comfortable with – those who don't know where to turn when it comes to design should look for clues in the types of pillow they prefer.

Personally, I love to embellish pillows. To me, the architectural space should be quiet and calm – hence my love of the neutral palette – but portable items, such as pillows, offer an opportunity to play with color, shape and texture. In part, it comes back to my love of textural contrast. A shiny satin band on a matte mohair pillow is satisfying both to the eye and to the touch, just as a horn button is

TOP LEFT Pillows are the perfect accessory to embellish – mother-of-pearl buttons are beautiful in their own right, but also add textural contrast. A neutral shade such as this has the advantage of sitting happily in most color schemes.

BELOW LEFT Accent color is an effective decorating tool and pillows are an ideal way of introducing it – as with this burnt orange pillow that takes center stage against its neutral companions. Horn buttons are used for ornamentation.

RIGHT Pillows are also visually pleasing when stacked, creating a composition on tables or beds. This arrangement of three, with a smaller one on top, is easy and effective. Note how banding has been used to link color and texture.

on a deep velvet fabric. But it is also because balance is so integral to my work, and the ornamentation of pillows is a way of linking certain elements within a room together. A pillow in a bedroom, for example, might be made up of three fabrics – one that relates to the headboard, one to the curtains and one that is unique to the pillow itself. When I make up a design board, the choice of pillow fabrics is a part of it just as flooring, furniture and paint colors are.

Pillows can be bought in every size and shape imaginable. Large floor ones immediately make a room feel laid-back and young, just as a row of uniformly square ones suggests order and structure. Bolster pillows are another useful addition to the palette – not only because they are comfortable in their own right for supporting the lower back or neck, but because you can prop other pillows against them. I particularly like those that offer further textural twists, such as woven rattan or leather versions.

Keep in mind though that pillows demand a certain level of maintenance. Ones that are saggy or misshapen make a room feel unloved. Natural feather fillings will droop over time, so you must remember to plump them up regularly to keep them looking good. You should also allow time to arrange them on the bed or sofa each morning – pillows left on the floor from the night before do nothing for the look of a room.

TOP LEFT A single linen pillow on a textured daybed harmonizes with the colors of the upholstery and throw. A wooden button has the same matte qualities as the fabric, cementing the feeling of quiet and unity.

MIDDLE LEFT Dark taupe and cream velvet pillows finished with mother-of-pearl buttons add a decorative touch to a bed. The contrast of light against dark is a simple way of drawing the eye and creating a pleasant visual effect.

BELOW LEFT These eggplant-colored pillows are made of silk organza which gives a slight luster to the surface. Mother-of-pearl buttons also have a reflective quality; they stand out beautifully against the richness of the fabric.

BELOW CENTER Because pillows are relatively small-scale objects, you can use them to play with fabrics that you might otherwise not think of choosing, such as this vintage velvet pillow in moss green with horn buttons that contrasts beautifully with crisp linen.

BELOW RIGHT Pillows can be used to provide shots of confident color, such as the burnt orange here. There is also a textural story because of the way the matte velvet plays against the shimmer of a black dyed goatskin throw.

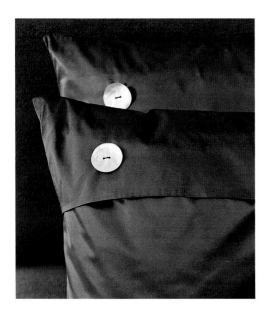

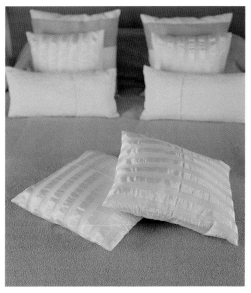

ABOVE When dressing a bed, consider pillows as a group rather than individually. Here the one placed centrally combines fabrics from both its companions, allowing the eye to gently travel forward from one color to the next.

BELOW LEFT Pillows are a useful device because they let you to introduce different moods into a room. Here, ones in rust and stone link directly to the padded blanket. The patterned designs help break up the otherwise neutral palette.

BELOW RIGHT Pillows can be used to create compositions on beds and sofas. These ones are all of the same off-white shade, but different shapes, patterns and textures mean they play against each other visually.

ABOVE A natural linen runner has been used down the cream bedspread of this single bed to add definition and interest. This has been accentuated by the corresponding runner down the pillow – both link to the color of the headboard.

LEFT Throws do not have to be used in the organic way their name suggests. Here a cashmere one has been carefully folded to create a runner effect down a bedroom chair. A simple rectangular pillow anchors the grid-like design.

OPPOSITE Runners can be used on dining tables to create a grid from which place settings are positioned and to give structure to the way the table is dressed. This silk one is placed centrally to focus attention on globe vases filled with miniature roseheads.

RUNNERS AND THROWS are a perennial

favorite with me because they help to underpin the grid structure within my designs. They are an easy way of introducing a linear dimension to a room, particularly when used in home furnishings such as bedcovers and pillows. They can also contribute to textural or color contrasts within the design. And they are an excellent way of reflecting seasonal changes – a warm felt runner, for example, has a different character entirely to a summery one made from voile.

Runners can be designed and sewn in as an integral part of an item, such as a headboard or bedspread. Or they can be a length of portable material that you arrange over an item of furniture to achieve a certain effect, perhaps on a table or over the back of a chair. It depends whether you want the runner as a permanent feature, or one that can be changed according to mood, season or function.

The important thing is to get the proportion right – both length and width. You can only do this by eye, but the secret is to achieve an effect whereby the runner is not so big that it dominates or so slim that it is

barely noticeable. You also need to think about whether the runners should all follow the same direction, or whether you want to accentuate the grid by having horizontal and vertical ones in place.

If runners denote structure, throws do the opposite. They are free-flowing and organic; it is no coincidence that they have the name they do. Throws are great for shaking up spaces that are almost too perfect, too symmetrical. They gently smudge sharp lines and rigid geometry. You can use them draped, folded, flat or hung. As with everything else in the room, have an awareness of the textural shiver they create – such as Indian paisley draped over a masculine, leather chair, or a fur blanket brushing against a limestone floor.

Throws also create a natural bridge between interiors and fashion, because items such as vintage shawls make perfect additions to an interiors scheme, particularly if they are made of luxurious materials such as silk, taffeta or cashmere. Ninety-five percent of fabrics in a room should connect in some way to each other, but it is exciting to have something in the design that is unique.

ACCESSORIES AND DISPLAY

Displaying objects

YOU CAN HAVE EVERYTHING IN YOUR HOME YOU EVER DREAMED OF,
BUT IF YOU DON'T TAKE THE TIME TO DISPLAY THE OBJECTS WITHIN
IT WITH CARE AND CONSIDERATION, IT WILL NEVER LOOK RIGHT.

We are all slaves to habit, but rooms can be totally transformed by the addition or removal of certain objects, paintings and flowers. That doesn't necessarily mean buying everything new – but rather thinking laterally and seeing that there are other possibilities for where things go than where they always go. I like to pack things away and then rediscover them in a year or so – you can unwrap something and appreciate it all over again for its form or texture. You need a different mindset when accessorizing: you must decide to change everything.

Start by clearing every surface – mantel, walls and tabletops. Now start again and try to avoid repeating the same arrangements you had previously.

Avoid too much symmetry. It is balance you should be striving for when it comes to display. Think of the room as a canvas on which you are trying to create the perfect still life. Never fill shelves from side to side. Decide on your center of focus and then radiate out from this point. The idea is to have different heights, textures, colors and widths, but within them to have a recurring theme that subtly draws them all together. Overlap some of the objects, so that some are slightly hidden and others take prime position. This technique of display gives a sense of mystery and depth to the finished composition.

Know when to stop. There is no point in having too many unique focal points – the eye will become confused and you will end up cluttering your home with too much stuff. My philosophy is to buy little and well.

GOLDEN RULES: DISPLAY

1 Display is a question of balance, so height is needed in one part of this room because width – the floating shelves – is in evidence in another. This simple cylindrical glass vase filled with buffalo grass and moss makes the perfect focal point on top of the cabinet.

2 Double-hung pictures of equal size also stress the vertical lines of the room, accentuating the idea of a grid. Do not make the mistake of hanging pictures too high – it is good to have something to look at when sitting as well as standing.

3 Rather than allowing table surfaces to become covered in paraphernalia, use them to create an interesting still life. Trays can be placed to create a canvas on which a composition is then arranged, with pairs of objects to emphasize symmetry.

4 Floating shelves are the perfect focal point for a complex arrangement of objects that includes glass, ceramics, books and paintings. The energy the objects generate when carefully balanced in terms of height, texture and color is visually very stimulating.

This harmonious living room has been carefully composed, from the well-balanced display on the floating shelves to the objects arranged in the tabletop tray. It follows the Zen principle that the eye should have somewhere soothing to rest.

CABINETS AND SIDETABLES
A piece of furniture on which you can display a group of objects or a collection of some kind makes an excellent focal point within a room, particularly if there is no fireplace or other architectural feature.

If your budget will allow, have a cabinet custom-made for the space. The advantage is not only that it will fit perfectly, but you can specify features such as integrated lighting. If you are planning to display a particular group of objects here, measure their height and width and work out the distance needed between shelves to house these specific items.

Do not be alarmed when you see the cabinet in place for the first time. When empty, it will look alarmingly large – out of proportion to the rest of the space. This is an illusion: once the shelves are filled, it will start to blend in with the rest of the room.

Sidetables are more akin to tabletops than cabinets. However, think about what the eye will see from a sitting position: sidetables are higher than tables so it is the profile of different forms that is important. Try to avoid having objects of the same scale or texture here – you need to play small against large, fat against thin, matte against gloss, smooth against rough, to create a stimulating effect. Finally, pay attention to the wall space behind: what you hang above the sidetable is as much a part of the composition as the objects upon it.

ABOVE A pair of dark wood cabinets brings symmetry. They are linked by a set of objects inspired by the sea, such as plaster shells, organic-shaped glass and globe vases of coral and sand.

OPPOSITE Cube-like shelves need careful dressing in order to keep balance and make connections between disparate objects. Glass globe vases of sand and coral are used to punctuate spaces between handblown glass, books and ceramic bowls of various sizes.

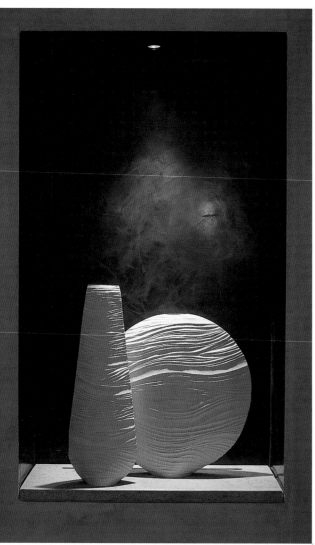

NICHES

NICHES are a skillful way of transforming a redundant space into a feature within a room. They can either be caused by imperfect architecture, in which case the addition of shelving is the best way of "flattening" a wall and making it appear as a continuous plane.

Or, a niche can be something consciously added to the design in order to create an area for display. Niches are not necessarily always carved out of a solid wall – they can become part of the boundary that separates one space from another.

Think of the niche as a piece of miniature theatre: you need a suitable backdrop against which to display your chosen objects well. Either illuminate the niche so that it is flooded with light – dramatic in a darkened room. Or light the arrangement with spots so that it is silhouetted against a dark velvety background. Do not leave it the same color as the rest of the wall – a textured finish, such as polished plaster, can be far more atmospheric. The proportions of a niche are the key to deciding what to display here – one tall, slim object perhaps, or a row of similarly shaped ones. Having made your choice, you now need to design shelving that fits both the selected objects and the space available. Floating shelves are often my preferred choice as they do not detract from the items they display.

Good lighting is also important. Niches are focal points so, in the evening particularly, they need lighting to draw the eye toward them. Backlighting provides a wash of atmospheric light, which will silhouette objects against it, while side lighting provides a uniform glow. A colored filter can be used on either to create a really dramatic effect. In addition you can use well-concealed low-voltage uplighters or downlighters to project beams of light onto the items displayed. An illuminated niche not only provides light to see these things by, but becomes part of the room's complete lighting design. At night, you may prefer to dim most of the lights, leaving niches to provide low-level ambient light.

Niches are best used for one or two striking objects or for a collection of identical ones. Do not confuse the look with too many items crammed together, or with ones of varying height and form. You do not have to spend much money to create a striking effect: once shelves and lighting are in place, something as simple as a row of Plexiglas boxes can create interest. However, if you do like to collect objects such as Murano glass or treen (small domestic wooden objects), the niche is an effective contemporary alternative to the glass-fronted display cabinet.

ABOVE The addition of niches introduces a sense of depth to this small dining room. The dark plaster finish and inset lighting makes a dramatic backdrop for textural ceramic craft objects.

RIGHT A guest bathroom has been made more glamorous with a custom-built wall of niches; shelves are deeper than the wall itself, creating an additional layer of interest. Eastern philosophy has inspired the perfectly balanced pairing of identical metal bowls.

OPPOSITE TOP This red niche adds accent color to a chic family kitchen. Blades of ornamental grass in test-tube vases introduces greenery to the room, while a row of tiny matching ceramic pots counterbalances the height, allowing the eye to be led both up and through.

OPPOSITE BELOW An L-shaped niche in the corner of a bedroom adds depth, while also making the ideal place for an installation of identical glass vases filled with sand and coral.

SHELVES

SHELVES are a design essential because they not only make it easier to keep a home neat, but create a natural display area within a room. Although it is possible to buy all sorts of ready-to-assemble shelving systems, I would always recommend having them custom-made to the space. The most elegant variety are floating shelves, that appear to hang unsupported – they are often my preferred choice as they do not detract from the items they display. As with niches (see pages 148-149), custom lighting can be used to add light at the back and sides or to highlight the objects on the shelves. As with framed pictures (see pages 154-155), shelves should be placed at a comfortable height so that they can be seen when either sitting or standing. Consider the size and height of the rest of the furniture within a room before fixing them in place.

There are essentially two approaches to dressing shelves. One is to use lots of identical objects that can be arranged in rows – either vertically or horizontally. However, you must be careful they do not end up totally symmetrical; a blank space can be the ideal way of breaking the flow. The second is to use a variety of objects, such as handblown glass, books, flowers and black-and-white photographs. Remember the principle of layering that is so important when creating a room: first you have the grid – the shelves – and then you need to add depth through the carefully considered display of other interesting design ingredients.

Look for balance not symmetry. You need to find a centerpoint to your arrangement – perhaps a unique focal point – and then work out from this, both up and down and side to side. Achieving the right combination of scale, color, texture and form can take a surprisingly long time, so simplify the process by repeating motifs throughout. For example, you may want three glass vases with flowers in your composition, but if so use three identical vases and three identical flowers. Too many variations will create a jumbled, confused effect.

Something else that is important to realize is that it is not only what you put on shelves, but the blank space around them.

RIGHT Creating a successful composition on shelves is dependent on understanding tension between objects. Here, the horizontal sculpture balances with the three pairs of vases filled with trimmed snake grass, while paintings that slightly overlap stress the energy between positive and negative spaces.

FAR LEFT When dressing shelves, keep things simple. Here a line of three globe vases filled with white hydrangea heads create an interesting still life against a dark wood background. The organic-shaped light stand breaks up the horizontal grid.

MIDDLE LEFT Stairways can be the perfect place to display art, but why not position it on shelves rather than hang it on the wall? Here, color photography enhanced by fiber-optic lighting makes an eye-catching focal point in an otherwise neutral space.

MIDDLE RIGHT Near-identical ceramic dishes have been positioned at different heights on shallow boxes to create additional interest on these floating shelves. The graphic shape of the anglepoise lamp becomes part of the whole tableau.

FAR RIGHT Specially commissioned floating shelves curve very slightly upwards at each end, challenging the idea that they must always be purely linear. Staineless-steel inserts add a subtly decorative touch, framing each vase of cream roses.

A shelf with nothing on it at all can be the perfect juxtaposition to one that is fairly full. One simple object centrally placed on a single shelf does not always require other companions. This sense of the importance of space between things, as well as the things themselves, is essential if you are going to be able to display objects effectively in your own home.

In design terms, this is described as positive and negative space: positive space is that which is filled by an object; negative space is the space around it. One of the reasons why I like to overlap pictures and other items on shelves is that it is a way of playing with the idea of positive and negative spaces.

Don't think only about the shelves, but about the space they inhabit. I like to make small but vital visual links between different elements in a room. So, for example, if there are black-and-white photographs propped up against shelves, I might also have a large black-and-white picture standing against the same wall. Similarly, a red flower in a vase on a shelf might reflect some bit of red introduced elsewhere in the room through a rug or throw.

Finally, don't allow your display to become too static. Just as you need to move furniture around sometimes in a room, or shake things up a bit by introducing a new set of pillows, so it is important to look at what you have on your shelves every six months or so and observe it with new eyes. The day when you look and no longer love what you see, is the day you must clear everything off the shelves and begin again.

FRAMED PICTURES

that you absolutely love should be the focal point of your room.

Lighting, colors and position of furniture can all be designed around them. There is a school of thought that thinks it is best to group disparate pictures together on a wall for maximum effect, but I would not support it. I think the effect is too confused and it becomes difficult to appreciate the merits of each piece. However, collections of art look fabulous when linked by scale, style and subject matter – such as black-and-white photography. I love this because it introduces a graphic element into a room and rarely fights with its surroundings. It is also possible to choose subject matter that has some sort of personal connection, be it a particular landscape, iconic figure or passion.

The monochrome nature of photography also helps when it comes to display. A horizontal line of photographs will reflect the grid design that underpins the design, while photographs propped up on shelves offer an informal way of challenging that rigidity. Scale again comes into play: one huge photographic image might dominate the room, but aim to link it to a series of smaller ones – grouped on another wall – for extra interest.

LEFT Art does not necessarily have to be positioned center stage in a room. Here, vintage Beatles memorabilia has been box-framed and hung together closely in a group of four. By placing it low on the wall it can be enjoyed at eye level by those sitting down.

OPPOSITE TOP RIGHT Think about how pictures interact with the furniture and objects around them. Here, bold black-and-white photography is hung low over a dark wood console, allowing the glass and silver objects on display to become part of the whole arrangement.

OPPOSITE BELOW LEFT The white frame of this huge photograph draws the eye to it, while also making a link to the white of the lamp shade and pillow. The arrangement of furniture also becomes part of the visual impact of this single piece.

OPPOSITE BELOW RIGHT Symmetry and asymmetry are important tools when displaying pictures. Here, a series of prints are hung along the wall in a uniform line. This is followed by a more unstructured arrangement, in order to break up the predictability of the frames.

MOUNTED OBJECTS

are an eye-catching alternative to conventional art. You can create your own focal point by taking three-dimensional pieces – particularly a series of identical ones – and displaying them well.

Whether it is something quirky, such as primitive masks, or something commonplace, such as boxes or pots, their impact will be made from the way they are grouped and the visual repetition of near-identical objects.

It is also a way of bringing your personality into a room, particularly if you choose to display a collection of artifacts that you have assembled yourself on your travels.

The world divides into two camps when it comes to creating mounted displays: making the room fit the installation, or the installation fit the room. There is no right or wrong here, but it is important to recognize which category you belong to in order to find the best solution. You can go in search of the perfect collection or unique focal point to finish off a look, but one of the most satisfying aspects to decorating is in creating a backdrop for a much-loved object or objects.

One of the reasons why I enjoy working with sculptural pieces like this is that they add a tactile element to a room as well as a visual one. Who could fail to want to run their fingers along carved wood or intricate gilt? The pleasure they give is doubled.

TOP LEFT Repetition of near-identical objects is an easy and effective way of creating visual drama. This installation of sculpture adds interest to the room, while the geometric way in which they are hung is part of the room's grid structure.

BELOW LEFT This mirror with its extravagant gilt frame becomes the unique focal point in an otherwise quietly neutral room. Something like this should not be centrally hung but placed in a more asymmetrical position in the space.

BELOW RIGHT This unusual stainless-steel fireplace with ripped-effect aperture is like a three-dimensional work of art. The abstract canvas above reinforces this idea – the juxtaposition of the two creates an unusual and stimulating still life.

OPPOSITE It is possible to take two separate objects and combine them together to create a new effect entirely. Here the cube of the fireplace is balanced by sculptural lights above of near-identical width. The vertical metal rods are integral to the fireplace.

TABLETOPS

are much more than a functional surface on which to place objects; they are a snapshot of you. Why cover a table with a jumbled assortment of newspapers, magazines and ashtrays, when with a little thought it can be transformed into something much more visually pleasing?

Of course they are a convenient surface on which to put things. But to me they are much more than that. They are not places for permanent displays, in the same way cabinets or shelves are, but an ever-changing landscape on which to put your signature.

Think of each table as a blank page on which to create a slice of visual drama. One of the easiest ways to achieve this transformation is by placing objects on a tray on the tabletop. A tray is like a portable canvas. It is also a way of introducing another textural layer into that corner of the room.

You can fill a tray with an assembly of repeated objects – something as inexpensive as polished green apples will do – and it can take on the energy of an art work. Or you can create an arrangement of different objects chosen for their contrasting sizes or textures. Books are another underrated design ingredient. I never grow tired of looking through glossy hardcovers filled with fantastic visual imagery. Your choice of tabletop reading reflects your personality, interests and taste, so why not have a few well chosen ones on hand that you have bought after seeing a favorite photography, painting or textile exhibition?

The eye enjoys being stimulated and it is fun to have small vistas such as this at eye-level to entertain people sitting down. Stretch the imagination and find new ways to display according to mood, season and occasion.

LEFT Trays are the perfect way of containing decorative items, which can then be displayed on tabletops. Balance is important, as shown here with the two cylinders of buffalo grass, echoed by a pair of glass candleholders and shallow ceramic bowls.

OPPOSITE These shallow wooden trays create a dark frame for carefully arranged gourds, which introduce wonderful color and texture into the room. A display like this takes a few minutes to perfect, so is easy to change on a weekly basis.

HERB RITTS WORK

HERB RITTS WORK

Robin Muir

Thames & Hudson

OPPOSITE A dark wood console behind a charcoal-covered sofa is the perfect place to introduce a bit of color – as with these three goldfish bowls of calla lilies with twisted stems. A tribal headrest at the far end – being of a similar height – balances the glass and flowers.

ABOVE Tabletops are ideal for introducing an additional grid of horizontals and verticals into a room. Here, a dark tray is set opposite two photographic books and linked to them by a globe vase of washed leaves. Also, tiny silver pots form a miniature grid of their own.

VASES AND VESSELS are like rooms within themselves; they are

what houses the flower or object. If you think of a vase in this way, it frees up the mind to come up with new, creative ways of furnishing it. One of my signature pieces is the globe glass bowl filled with white sand and coral or filled with nothing more than a coil of natural rope – it not only looks fabulous, but is ideal in less-used areas of the home, such as a guest suite or in a vacation home where it would be impractical to maintain fresh flowers.

The rule of thumb I use when choosing flowers for my interiors is either to buy a lot or a little, and this naturally influences the choice of vase. You need something large for dramatic flowers with star quality and long stems, but you also need containers on a much more modest scale. If you find a good shape – such as a clear box, globe bowl, test-tube vase or tall cylinder – then buy them in quantity. One rose bud in a test tube will go unnoticed, but a row of ten becomes a striking installation piece.

When I find vases I love for their own sake, I rarely fill them with flowers but leave them empty. Wonderful handblown glass vessels, for example, have such a beautiful organic shape in their own right they need nothing else added. You have to make a simple choice as to where you want the eye to fall: on the flowers or on the vase.

ABOVE It is not always necessary to fill vessels and vases with fresh flowers and greenery. White rope is an unexpected companion to oversized brandy glasses, but in fact the textures work well together and the pale rope stands out against the dark tones of the wood.

OPPOSITE TOP LEFT Vases of colored glass are beautiful in their own right and need nothing in them. Here, the yellow tones echo those of the blind to the right. A purple and yellow vessel punctuates the space between these two elements.

OPPOSITE TOP RIGHT This sculptural oversized ceramic vase, filled with white carnations, creates a pleasing still life in a corner of a living room, particularly when juxtaposed against billowing white curtains. The tiny glass dish to the left plays on the idea of scale.

MIDDLE LEFT Glass of different hues is the perfect way of introducing small amounts of color into an otherwise neutral room. Here, shelves have been painted to match the taupe of the vase, while the red tint provides an interesting contrast.

MIDDLE RIGHT Goldfish bowls of white sand and coral not only provide a decorative focal point in a shelving display, but are easier to maintain than fresh flowers. This makes them ideal for use in locations such as summer homes or guest suites.

BELOW LEFT Vessels come in many different textures, making them perfect for introducing textural contrast. Here the rough wooden surface of a vase plays against the shininess of a ceramic dish to its right and glass to its left.

BELOW RIGHT Two oversized tawny glass bottles were chosen for their size and square shape. They are filled with dried leaves, which create interesting shadows and outlines within.

TOP ROW FAR LEFT The same flowers can be presented differently to create added interest in a group arrangement. Here, tall stems of red amaryllis and pussy willow burst from the taller vases, while the stems are cut short for the middle vase, to echo its smaller stature.

BOTTOM ROW FAR LEFT Traditional roses have been given a contemporary twist by wrapping them in ligularia leaves to frame individual flower heads. Groups of a single variety of flower in identical vases often have more visual impact than lots of different flower types in a single vase.

BOTTOM ROW LEFT This perfectly balanced composition comprises two glass vases of red roses with quite different personalities. In one, they are cut short at the stem so that they float in water. In the other, their long-stems tilt at a jaunty angle over the edge of the globe vase.

TOP ROW SECOND FROM LEFT Trays are an unusual but effective way of displaying flowers. Here a simple Plexiglas one has been layered with white calla lilies to produce a tabletop arrangement. Note how the cut stems have been laid across the container to create a grid.

ABOVE Flowers can be used to produce an installation piece, as with the three big silver urns of white primrose in this wet room. Not only does the metallic surface contrast beautifully with the matte stone walls, but the white flowers stand out graphically against its dark tone.

TOP RIGHT A huge white pot of orchids – one of a pair – is an eye-catching contrast to the dark wood floor on which it stands. Black-and-white photography is hung low so that it becomes part of the composition.

FRESH FLOWERS can either be extroverted or introverted, a centerpiece

or quietly harmonious in a room setting. There are some that have an architectural quality that I never tire of – like calla lilies and orchids – and others that are there to introduce spot color, such as tightly budded red roses. I admit to being ruthless when working with flowers – I love them best before they open; once they do, I throw them out. I also have no qualms about cutting the stems cruelly short so that they can be arranged in linear ways, such as in a row of test-tube vases.

The other important thing to recognize is that "flowers" is now a term that encompasses all kinds of organic produce including bulbs, fruit, vegetables, leaves, grass and moss. If you get up early to visit a flower market, take a good look around the vegetable market too. Apples, artichokes, red onions and lychees look fantastic with polished skins. Celery, cauliflower and artichokes offer wonderful shapes with which to work.

From a design point of view, flowers offer a way of introducing ideas of scale into a room. It may be that I will put one huge installation of cut roses in one corner of a bedroom, for example, then take two of the flower heads and place them in a Plexiglas box on a bedside table. It creates a visual link from one corner of the room to the other, but in a wonderfully subtle way.

Consider how to group flowers effectively. Here, white tulips tied with stems work beautifully as a pair, each arrangement reflecting the height of its container. The green glass dish to the right draws out the colors in this still life perfectly.

OPPOSITE Flowers should be part of a room's design, not separate from it. Here tall-stemmed calla lilies echo the organic metal waves created by these sculptural floor lights. The height of both lights and flowers is in direct contrast to the low-level of the furniture.

Address book

SPECIALTY FABRICS

ABBOTT & BOYD
8 Chelsea Harbour
Design Centre
London SW10 OXE
Tel: +44 (0) 20 7351 9985
www.abbottandboyd.co.uk
Fabrics and wallpaper.

ALEX BEGG & COMPANY
17 Viewfield Road
Ary, Scotland KA8 AHJ
Tel: +44 (0) 12 92267 615
www.beggscotland.com
Cashmere.

ALTON BROOKE
Unit 2/25 Chelsea
Harbour Design Centre
London SW10 OXE
Tel: +44 (0) 20 7376 7008
www.alton-brooke.co.uk
Specialty fabrics and rugs.

BENNETT SILKS
Elijah Slocum
8360 Melrose Avenue
Los Angeles, CA 90069
Tel: 323 655 1263
www.bennett-silks.co.uk
Satin, silks.

BERGAMO FABRICS
979 Third Avenue
17th Floor
New York, NY 10022
Tel: 212 888 3333
www.bergamofabrics.com

BILL AMBERG
The Workshop
31 Elkstone Road
London W10 5NT
Tel: +44 (0) 20 8960 2000
www.billamberg.com
Leather, vellum.

BRUNSCHWIG & FILS
75 Virginia Road
North White Plains
New York 10603
Tel: 800 538 1880
www.Brunschwig.com

CREATION BAUMANN
114 North Center Avenue
Rockville Center, NY 11570
Tel: 516 764 7431
www.creationbaumann.com
Contemporary textured fabrics.

DESIGNERS GUILD
3 Latimer Place
London W10 6QT
Tel: +44 (0) 20 7893 7700
www.designersguild.com
Cotton.

DONGHIA
485 Broadway
New York, NY 10013
Tel: 212 925 2777
www.donghia.com
Contemporary furniture, textured fabrics.

ENZO DEGLI ANGIUONI SPA
Via G. Fara 26
20030 Birago di Lentate
Milan

Tel: +39 0362 53101
www.edaspa.com
Fabric.

F.R. STREET
Frederick House
Hurricane Way
Wickford Business Park
Wickford
Essex SS11 8YB
Tel: +44 (0) 1268 766 677
www.streets.co.uk
Calico, linen, scrim.

FOX LINTON
2nd Floor,
8-10 Chelsea Harbour
Design Centre
London SW10 OXE
Tel: +44 (0) 20 7351 9908
www.foxlinton.com
Sheers, silk, suede.

HOLLAND & SHERRY, INC
150 East 58th Street
14th Floor
New York, NY 10155
Tel: 212 758 1911
www.hollandandsherry.com
Wool, cashmere.

I.D. COLLECTION
Dallas Design Collection
1025 N. Stemmons Freeway
Suite 745
Dallas, TX 75207
Tel: 214 698 0226

J. ROBERT SCOTT
430 North Wells Street
Chicago, IL 60610
Tel: 312 527 2907
www.jrobertscott.com
Contemporary furniture, silks, textured
fabrics.

**JAB INTERNATIONAL
FURNISHINGS**
Stroheim & Romann
155 East 56th Street
New York, NY 10022
Tel: 212 486 1500
www.jab.de
Upholstery fabrics.

JOHN BOYD TEXTILES LTD
Higher Flax Mills
Torbay Road
Castle Cary
Somerset BA7 7DY
Tel: +44 (0) 1963 350451
www.johnboydtextiles.co.uk
Horsehair fabric and manufacturers.

KRAVET
225 Central Avenue South
Bethpage, NY 11714
Tel: 516 293 2000
www.kravet.com
Upholstery chenilles.

LEE JOFA
979 Third Avenue
New York, NY 10022
Tel: 212 688 0444
www.leejofa.com

LIBECO LAGAE
Tielstraat 112
8760 Meulebeke
Belgium
Tel: +32 (0) 5 148 8921
www.libeco.be
Linen.

MALABAR
31-33 The South Bank Business Centre
Ponton Road
London SW8 5BL
Tel: +44 (0) 20 7501 4200
www.malabar.co.uk

MONKWELL LTD
227 Kings Road
London SW3 5EJ
Tel: +44 (0) 20 7823 3294
www.monkwell.com
Furnishing fabrics and wallpaper.

NICHOLAS HASLAM LTD
12-14 Holbein Place
London SW1W 8NL
Tel: +44 (0) 20 7730 8623
www.nicholashaslam.com
Chenile, moleskin, contemporary furniture.

OSBORNE & LITTLE
979 Third Avenue
Suite 520
New York, NY 10022
www.osborneandlittle.com
Fabric and wallpaper.

OLICANA TEXTILES LTD
Brook Mills,
Carr Lane,
Slaithwaite,
Huddersfield HD7 5BQ
Tel: +44 (0) 1484 847666
sales@olicana.co.uk
Cotton.

PIERRE FREY
12 East 33rd Street
New York, NY 10016
Tel: 212 213 3099
www.pierrefrey.com
Furnishing fabric.

RANDOLPH & HEIN
101 Henry Adams Street
Suite 1
San Francisco, CA 94103
Tel: 415 864 3550
www.randolphhein.com

ROGER OATES DESIGN
Head Office
The Long Barn
Eastnor, Ledbury
Herefordshire HR8 1EL
Tel: +44 (0) 1531 631611
www.rogeroates.com
Linen.

RUSSELL & CHAPPLE
68 Drury Lane
Covent Garden
London WC2B 5SP
Tel: +44 (0) 20 7836 7521
www.russellandchapple.co.uk
Calico, linen scrim.

SABINA FAY BRAXTON
38/40 Avenue
Jean-Jaures
94110 Arcueil
France
Tel: +33 (0) 4657 1162
sabinafay@wanadoo.fr
Hand-colored and specialty fabrics.

SAHCO HESSLEIN LTD
Hirtenwiesenstr. 8c.
90475 Nurnberg
Germany
Tel: + 49 (0) 911 83 23 58
www.sahco-hesslein.com
Mohair, sheers and voiles.
Textured fabrics.

SCALAMANDRÉ
222 East 59th Street
New York, NY 10022
Tel: 212 980 1002
www.scalamandre.com

STARK CARPET
979 Third Avenue
11th Floor
New York, NY 10022
Tel: 212 758 4342
www.starkcarpet.com

TELIO & CIE
5800 St. Denis
Suite 502
Montreal H3S 3L5
Tel: 514 271 4607
www.telio.com

V.V. ROULEAUX
54 Sloane Square
London SW1W 8AX
Tel: +44 (0) 20 7730 3125
www.vvrouleaux.com
Ribbon.

WALLS & PAINTS

FIRED EARTH LTD
Tywford Mill
Oxford Road
Adderbury
Oxfordshire OX17 3HP
Tel: +44 (0) 12 9581 2088
www.firedearth.com
Kelly Hoppen paint range.

ZOFFANY
979 3rd Avenue
New York, NY 10022
Tel: 800 395 8760
www.zoffany.com
Wallpapers, paints and fabrics.

FLOORING & CUSTOM FINISHES

ABC CARPET & HOME
888 Broadway
New York, NY 10021
Tel: 212 966 4700
www.abchome.com

JANOS SPITZER FLOORING COMPANY
131 West 24th Street
New York, NY 10011
Tel: 212 627 1818

LIMESTONE GALLERY LTD
Arch 47, South Lambeth Road
London SW8 1SS
Tel: + 44 (0) 20 7735 8555
www.limestonegallery.com
Bespoke stonework for bathrooms,
kitchens and staircases. Solid stone
bath tubs.

THE RUG COMPANY
124 Holland Park Avenue
London W11 4UE
Tel: + 44 (0) 20 7229 5148
www.therugcompany.co.uk
Rugs and carpets.

WALKER ZANGER
37 East 20th Street
New York, NY 10003
www.walkerzanger.com

FURNITURE & ACCESSORIES

ARMANI CASA
157 N. Robertson Blvd.
Los Angeles, CA 90048
Tel: 310 248 2440
www.armanicasa.com

B & B ITALIA
150 East 58th Street
New York, NY 10155
Tel: 800 872 1697
www.bebitalia.it
Contemporary furniture.

BO CONCEPT
The Shops at Gainey Village
8787 N. Scottsdale Road
Scottsdale, AZ 85253
Tel: 480 443 0900
www.boconcept.com
Danish furniture design and accessories.

CASAMILANO
1-20036 Medea
Milano
Via dei celuschi 8
Italia
Tel: +39 0362 340 499
www.ca samilanohome.com
Furniture.

CASSINA
55 East 56th Street
New York, NY 10022
Tel: 800 770 3568
www.cassinausa.com

CHEETAH DESIGN LTD
Maytham Farm Oast
Rolvenden Layne
Kent TN17 4QA
Tel: +44 (0) 1797 270149
www.cheetahdesign.net
Contemporary furniture and lighting.

DAVID LINLEY & CO LTD
60 Pimlico Road
London SW1W 8LP
Tel: +44 (0) 20 7730 7300

www.davidlinley.com
Furniture and custom-joinery.

DOMUS DESIGN COLLECTION
181 Madison Avenue
New York, NY 10016
Tel: 212 685 0800
www.ddcnyc.com

FLEXFORM
Nova Studio International
150 East 58th Street
New York, NY 10155
Tel: 212 421 1220
www.flexformusa.com

KARTELL
170 North East 40th Street
Miami, FL 33137
Tel: 305 573 4010
www.kartell.com

KELLY HOPPEN SHOP
175-177 Fulham Road
London SW3 6JW
Tel: +44 (0) 20 7351 1910
www.kellyhoppen.com
Kelly Hoppen interior design shop.

MAURICE VILLENCY, INC.
200 East 57th Street
New York, NY 10022
Tel: 212 725 4840
www.mauricevillency.com

MINOTTI CUCINE SPA
31 Via Napoleone
37015 Ponton di Sant Ambrogio di
Valpolicella
Verona
Italy
Tel: +39 045 6860 464
www.minotticucine.it
Contemporary furniture.

MODENATURE
59 Rue de Seine
75006
Paris
Tel: +33 1 53103170

www.modenature.com
Contemporary furniture.

MODERN LIVING
8775 Beverly Blvd.
Los Angeles, CA 90048
www.modernliving.com

OKA DIRECT LTD
809 Fulham Road (Mimosa Street)
London SW6 5HE
Tel: +44 (0) 20 7348 7090
www.okadirect.com
Furniture.

PHILIPP PLEIN
Hebelstrasse
D-90491
Nuernberg
Germany
Tel: +49 (0) 180 546 8374
www.philipp-plein.com
Contemporary furniture.

POLIFORM
150 East 58th Street
11th Floor
New York, NY 10155
Tel: 212 421 1220
www.poliform.com
Furniture.

SNAP DRAGON (LEONIE LEE LTD)
247 Fulham Road
London SW3 6HY
Tel: +44 (0) 20 7376 8889
www.snap-dragon.net
Chinese antique furniture.

THE TERENCE CONRAN SHOP
407 East 59th Street
New York, NY 10022
Tel: 212 755 9079
www.conran.com

LIGHTING

ARTEMIDE
9006 Beverly Blvd.
West Hollywood, CA 90048
tel: 800 359 7040

LOUIS POULSEN LIGHTING INC.
3260 Meridan Parkway
Fort Lauderdale, FL 33331
tel: 954 349 2525
www.louispoulsen.com

URBAN ARCHAEOLOGY
143 Franklin Street
New York, NY 10013
Tel: 212 431 4646
www.urbanarchaeology.com

WINDOW TREATMENTS

ROBERT ALLEN
New York
Tel: 800 240 8189
www.robertallendesign.com

THE BRADLEY COLLECTION LTD
Lion Barn
Maitland Road
Needham Market
Suffolk IP6 8NS
Tel: +44 (0) 14 4972 2724
www.bradleycollection.co.uk
Curtain poles and finials.

DRAKS SHUTTERS
Unit 316, Heyford Park
Upper Heyford
Oxfordshire OX6 3HA
Tel: +44 (0) 18 6923 2989
www.sin.be
Shutters.

SILENT GLISS LTD
Star Lane
Margate
Kent CT9 4EF
Tel: +44 (0) 1843 863571
www.silentgliss.co.uk
Window treatments including Kelly
Hoppen Collection.

SMITH & NOBLE
Tel: 800 248 8888
www.smithandnoble.com

KITCHENS & BATHROOMS

AGAPE
Via XX Settembre 29A
46100 Mantova
Italy
Tel: +39 0376 369 709
www.agapedesign.it
Bathroom fittings.

ALTERNATIVE PLANS LTD
9 Hester Road
London SW11 4AN
Tel: +44 (0) 20 7924 1164
www.alternative-plans.co.uk
Kitchens and bathrooms.

BOFFI
1344 4th Street
Santa Monica, CA 90401
Tel: 310 458 9300
www.boffi.com
Kitchens and bathrooms.

POGGENPOHL
145 US Hwy 46 West
Suite 200
Wayne, NJ 07470
Tel: 973 812 8900
www.poggenpohl-usa.com

STONE FOREST
213 South St. Francis Drive
Sanat Fe, NM 87501
Tel: 888 682 2987
www.stoneforest.com

WATERFRONT
6-7 Hale Trading Estate
Lower Church Lane
Tipton
West Midlands DY4 7PQ
Tel: +44 (0) 121 520 5346
www.waterfrontbathrooms.com
Kelly Hoppen taps and bathroom fittings.

ACCESSORIES & DISPLAY

CHRISTIE'S
20 Rockerfeller Plaza
New York, NY 10020
Tel: 212 636 2000
www.christies.com
Auction house for unique and beautiful
pieces.

GIBSON MUSIC LTD
Unit 8
50 Sulivan Road
London SW6 3DX
Tel: +44 (0) 20 7384 2270
www.gibson-music.com
Musical instruments and music.

MICHAEL HOPPEN PHOTOGRAPHY
3 Jubilee Place
London SW3 3TD
Tel: +44 (0) 20 7352 3649
Website: www.michaelhoppengallery.com
Photography.

SOTHEBY'S
1334 York Avenue
New York, NY 10021
Tel: 212 606 7000
www.sothebys.com
Decorative art and design pieces.

KELLY HOPPEN DESIGN SUPPLIERS

CENTURY FURNITURE
401 11th Street N.W.
Hickory, NC 28601
Tel: 828 328 1851
www.centuryfurniture.com
Kelly Hoppen furniture

CHESNEY'S, INC.
979 Third Avenue, Suite 244
New York, NY 10022
Tel: 866 840 0609
www.chesneys-usa.com
Kelly Hoppen fireplace mantels

CRAIG & ROSE
Halbeath Industrial Estate, Unit 8
Crossgates Road
Dunfermline
Fife KY11 7EG
Tel: +44 (0) 1383 740011
www.craigandrose.com
Kelly Hoppen paints

HOLLAND & SHERRY
9-10 Saville Row
London W1S 3PF
Tel: +44 (0) 20 7437 0404
www.hollandandsherry.co.uk
Kelly Hoppen fabric collection

KELLY HOPPEN INTERIORS
2 Munden Street
London W14 0RH
Tel: +44 (0) 20 7471 3350
www.kellyhoppen.com
Interior design studio

KELLY HOPPEN STORE
175-177 Fulham Road
London SW3 6JW
Tel: +44 (0) 20 7351 1910
www.kellyhoppen.com
Interior design store

NEIMAN MARCUS
390 San Lorenzo Avenue
Coral Gables, FL 33146
Tel: 786 999 1000
www.neimanmarcus.com
Kelly Hoppen boutique

NEIMAN MARCUS
150 Stockton Street
San Francisco, CA 94108
Tel: 414 362 3900
www.neimanmarcus.com
Kelly Hoppen boutique

SFERRA BROTHERS
15 Mayfield Avenue
Edison, NJ 08837
Tel: 732 225 6290
www.sferralinens.com/kellyhoppen
Kelly Hoppen bed linens

TRANS-OCEAN IMPORT COMPANY
1 Barker Avenue
White Plains, New York 10601
Tel: 914 949 5656
www.transocean.com
Kelly Hoppen rugs

WATERFRONT
6-7 Hale Trading Estate
Lower Church Lane
Tipton
West Midlands DY4 7PQ
Tel: +44 (0) 121 520 5346
www.waterfrontbathrooms.com
Kelly Hoppen bathroom fixtures

WEDGWOOD
Barlaston
Stoke-on-Trent ST12 9ES
Tel: +44 (0) 1782 204141
www.wedgwood.com
Kelly Hoppen china

WOOL CLASSICS
Chelsea Harbour Design Centre
Chelsea Harbour
London SW10 0XE
Tel: +44 (0) 20 7349 0090
www.chelsea-harbour.co.uk
Kelly Hoppen carpets

Index

Acknowledgments

Firstly I would like to thank all my clients who have allowed me back into their homes to photograph the finished results. Without your generous co-operation this book would not have been possible. A big thank you to my team at KHI. Thank-you Lisa Gibbs; Fabienne Finkelstein; Francesca Rossi; Didi Tapanlis; James Nielsen; Richard Stevens, Alex Bennaim, Avni Avram and Heloise Askew for running these projects as smoothly as they do. A special thanks to Olivia Lewzey, who is an angel, for her constant support and for being a back bone to KHI. Michael Lindsay-Watson – you are my hero and pillar of strength. Kim Jackson whose vision, spirit and inspiration is testimony on every page. Thank you. A warm thank you to John Carter for your everlasting creativity and commitment to my clients and me. Rica – for keeping all our lives in order. Without you life would be awful. Helen Chislett for interpreting my creative world so meticulously. Vincent Knapp for photographing my work exactly how I conceived the design. Thank you to Lawrence Morton for his creative design and to Bella Pringle for editing the book with such care. Thanks to Luciano Giubelli for working with me to create extraordinary gardens. Doreen Scott – a magician with fabric.

Picture Credits:
Grant at C Best - for generously lending us vases.
Peter Adler – we appreciate the endless support for all the shoots pg 16, 17
Architects: Koski Solomon Ruthven
Bottom left 24 34,35, 38, 39,42 top right 43, 45 bottom left 48, 49, 53 bottom left, 55 54 top left and top right, 66 bottom left, 84 and 85, 102 118, 119, 120, 121 middle top, 122 middle top left, 125 top left, 126, 149 top.